EDIBLE PERENNIAL GARDENING

Growing Successful Polycultures in Small Spaces

ANNI KELSEY

PERMANENT PUBLICATIONS

Published by
Permanent Publications
Hyden House Ltd
The Sustainability Centre
East Meon
Hampshire GU32 1HR
United Kingdom
Tel: 0844 846 846 4824 (local rate UK only)
         or +44 (0)1730 823 311
Fax: 01730 823 322
Email: enquiries@permaculture.co.uk
Web: www.permanentpublications.co.uk

Distributed in the USA by
Chelsea Green Publishing Company, PO Box 428, White River Junction, VT 05001
www.chelseagreen.com

Anni Kelsey's blog: http://annisveggies.wordpress.com

Photographs © Anni Kelsey, unless stated otherwise

Illustrations by Emma Lawrence, www.emmalawrence.com

Designed by Two Plus George Limited, wwwTwoPlusGeorge.co.uk

Index by Amit Prasad, 009amit@gmail.com

Printed in the UK by Cambrian Printers, Aberystwyth

All paper from FSC certified mixed sources

The Forest Stewardship Council (FSC) is a non-profit international
organisation established to promote the responsible management of
the world's forests. Products carrying the FSC label are independently
certified to assure consumers that they come from forests that are
managed to meet the social, economic and ecological needs of
present and future generations.

British Library Cataloguing-in-Publication Data
A catalogue record for this book is available from the British Library

ISBN 978 1 85623 149 7

CONTENTS

The Author   vii

Acknowledgements   viii

Foreword   ix

Introduction
Anticipation   1

Chapter 1
**Setting an Objective –
find and grow as many perennial vegetables as possible**   5

Starting points   5
Be realistic but push the boundaries of possibility   6
Definitions   11
What is special about perennial vegetables?   11
Are there any disadvantages?   13
Find and grow as many perennial vegetables as possible   13
Principles   15

Chapter 2
**Foundations and Underlying Themes –
permaculture, forest gardening and natural farming**   19

Permaculture   19
Edible forest gardening   20
Masanobu Fukuoka and natural farming   22
Synthesis   24
A wider context   24
What are we 'transitioning' towards?   25

Chapter 3

Living Soil and Plant Nutrition 27

The basics of soil structure 27
Healthy soil is alive 28
Soil food webs 32
Dead food web 32
Living food web 32
Plants need the right nutrients 33
The gardener's part 33

Chapter 4

Growing in Polycultures – Diversity by Design 37

What is a polyculture? 37
The advantages of polycultures 38
The elements of polycultures 38
Plant size, shape and form 41

Chapter 5

Choosing Perennial Vegetables – Part One 43

Selecting suitable perennials 44
Perennial leafy greens and shoots 45
Perennial green vegetables – cabbage family 47
Other perennial kales 51
Perennial green vegetables – other plant families 52
Perennial onions 56
Perennial roots and tubers 64

Chapter 6

Choosing Perennial Vegetables – Part Two 75

Annuals that can be grown as perennials 75
Annual greens as perennials 78
Other useful annual greens 80
Annual roots grown as perennials 81
Perennials I would have liked to be able to grow better 82
Miscellaneous other perennial vegetables 86
Flowers 91

Chapter 7
Cooking with New Foods
93

Eating your perennial vegetables   93
Hearty chick pea and kale soup   94
Kale and leek colcannon   95
Kale with ginger, garlic and chilli   96
Wild rocket soup   97
Roasted perennial root vegetables   97

Chapter 8
Plants to Complete a Polyculture
99

Tall plants   100
Medium height plants   102
Ground cover and low plants   104
Climbers   107
Nitrogen fixers   109
Flowers   109

Chapter 9
Pathways to Polyculture
111

Starting points and general principles   111
Planning a polyculture   113
Creating edible polycultures   113
Size and scale   115

Chapter 10
Site Selection and Preparation
117

Where to grow perennial vegetables   117
Site preparation and initial fertility   118
Establishing the patch and ongoing fertility   121
Raising plants from seed   123
Fruit trees, bushes and forest gardens   124
Potted polycultures   125
Storing produce   125

Chapter 11
'Managing' a Polyculture

127

On balance   127
Principles   128
How does this work in practice?   129
'Weeding'   131
Mineral accumulators   134
Nitrogen fixers   134
Pests and diseases   135
Fertility   138
The 'do nothing' vegetable patch   139
Productivity   139
Edible landscaping   140
Resilience   141

Chapter 12
Reflection

143

Appendix 1
Table of perennial vegetable plants
147

Appendix 2
Suppliers of seeds and perennial vegetable plants
152

Appendix 3
Books, websites and blogs
155

Appendix 4
Dynamic accumulator plants
160

Appendix 5
Enzyme co-factors in physiological processes
161

Index
162

The Author

Anni Kelsey has been aware of environmental issues since finding a Greenpeace leaflet at school in 1972. She studied Geography and graduated from Aberystwyth University with a first class degree in 1990. This led to research and project management work in economic and community development and urban regeneration schemes. Looking for something more meaningful and life affirming she then trained in reflexology, Bowen technique, and nutritional medicine and says, "I have learned how to keep myself and my family very healthy!" Her passion lies with forest gardening, permaculture and The Transition Movement. Anni currently works as an administrator, has two grown up children, and spends her spare time outside in the garden or countryside, reading, researching and writing.

This book is dedicated to its readers

Acknowledgements

Many people have contributed to this book without being aware that they have done so. They are the writers and bloggers that I have been avidly reading. To undertake research and complete this project I have needed much more than mere technical details of rare and unusual plants and seeds, where to buy them and how to grow them; I have needed inspiration. In particular I have found it in the blogs of people who are looking into the future and working out in very practical ways how they can make their bit of difference. Whether by living closer to nature, growing their own food, helping their communities in Transition, living by the principles of permaculture – I have found masses of inspiration which has been invaluable to helping me focus on the task of working out how to grow an edible perennial garden in the context of a changing world.

A massive thank you must go to the team at Permanent Publications and in particular to Maddy and Tim Harland who live by the ethics of the permaculture message that they have done so much to spread. I am indebted to Maddy's recognition of the potential for a book about perennial vegetables and her continuing enthusiasm and support throughout, and particularly thank Tim for his meticulous approach and eye for detail.

I am indebted to Emma Lawrence who has produced the drawings contained in this book. Starting from my basic and scrappy sketches she has done her own research into the topics illustrated and with immense care and thoughtfulness turned them into lovely pictures that show exactly what I had hoped for.

It has also been good to have the support of friends and family who have taken such an interest over the past few years.

Most importantly there is my beloved partner Pat, who makes all the difference to everything. She has given me never ending support and encouragement. In the early days (when it was not at all clear that the project would be as successful as it has been) it must have been a trial to see her once respectable garden turned over to riotous polycultures which included dandelions and nettles. However she has just reminded me that it was her idea to extend the area under cultivation to give more space for my experiments! She has also helped to find imaginative ways to cook and eat the unusual foods that now grace our table.

FOREWORD

Learning to produce food from perennials is a matter of critical importance for the 21st century. Perennials sequester carbon and help slow climate change, and can prevent erosion, slow and infiltrate rainfall, and reduce labor and inputs. Growing those perennial crops in polycultures adds even more benefits, and can give birth to productive novel ecosystems in our farms and gardens.

For those of us in cold climates, however, there is much to learn before these systems are ready for scaling up. Few nurseries and seed companies stock perennial crops (Kelsey lists many such sources). Learning to grow and build polycultures around perennial food plants can be difficult. Perhaps the hardest thing is learning to incorporate these crops in our diets on a daily basis.

What our movement needs now is to hear the stories of the innovative growers who are learning what perennial crops grow well for them, how they are managing them, and how they are combining them in polycultures. Anni Kelsey's *Edible Perennial Gardening: Growing Successful Polycultures* is filling this important need.

Kelsey has almost a decade of experience growing perennial vegetables in polycultures. She reports on her experiences – what grows easily, what is killed by frost, what the slugs and cabbage moths go after. Permaculture is sometimes accused of oversimplifying and making it all sound too easy. Here Kelsey provides the antidote, sharing mistakes and failures in the context of her overall success in growing a diverse blend of long-lived vegetable crops and companion species.

Particularly of value are her thoughts on managing for balance in polycultures, and the importance of monitoring and guiding succession in the edible perennial garden. These observations come from real personal experience and are invaluable to all of us in this movement.

Even better, Kelsey has tracked labor by month and yields. To my knowledge this is the very first time anyone in the movement has been able to say how many kilograms of perennial food she produced with so many hours of labor. I'm most grateful to her for this contribution to our movement and hope she will inspire others to do the same.

ERIC TOENSMEIER
Author of *Paradise Lot* and *Perennial Vegetables,* co-author of *Edible Forest Gardens*
Holyoke, Massachusetts, USA
October 2013

INTRODUCTION
Anticipation

Looking towards a sustainable future when a polyculture of perennial vegetables is as familiar a feature of our gardening landscape as the conventional vegetable patch.

I have always loved gardening. It is one of my very favourite things. However I used to feel that at best I was only just keeping on top of things, the garden always had more energy to put into growing than I did to put into its control, and it never took a day off. So it was in the summer of 2005 as I once again hacked back the excessive growth in the shrub borders that the thought struck me how good would it be if this exuberant greenery was all edible? Clearly the garden was capable of producing vast quantities of greenery, would it not be wonderful if I could eat it? What a lot of work it would save!

Allowing the whimsy to take flight I imagined a garden of plenty where the vegetables regrew each year and all I would have to do would be to go out and gather them. I am a bit prone to fanciful notions but thought I would check this out anyway and after a bit of internet searching I was reading about edible forest gardens. I was hooked.

What I read about that evening enchanted me. Imagine a forest of food, a place where food virtually grows itself with edible fruits, nuts and leaves growing all around. Who wouldn't want one? A place of serenity, beauty and fertile bounty where balance is achieved and the plants are diverse and healthy. Well chosen and balanced plantings would reduce upkeep to a minimum and best of all many of the food plants in this magical place would be perennials returning year after year. Was this merely a utopian dream or a whimsy? No, this is real. Gardens like this, designed by people, but directed by nature are full of surprises.

Although forest gardening captivated me instantaneously I have been following the initial dream for nearly a decade now, chasing it down into a reality that I can see and eat. I have been on a journey of discovery and change in the course of which I have learned so much that is exciting, and experienced a revolution in my view and understanding of many things.

The one drawback that I could see initially in the concept of forest gardens was that without sufficient room to grow more than a few trees, there did not seem to be much choice of perennial foods. I was particularly interested in vegetables, but at that time the choice was rather limited and not that exciting. Thus began a quest to search out perennial vegetables — looking for any that would be useful, interesting and palatable. I hoped what I found might provide a viable alternative or addition to established vegetables and that they would come up year after year just for the picking, with minimal input from me.

This book is the result; it is the book I would have liked to have had in my hand the evening I first read of forest gardening. I wish I had known then what I know now — that perennial vegetables do exist and can be grown without difficulty. I believe that they are potentially so useful I wish I could transplant what I have learned into the heads of all gardeners.

On the journey I have also learned to garden in a way that is about collaborating (co-labouring) with nature and not in any way about control over her. I initially intended to write primarily about the perennial vegetables themselves, but as it has turned out they are perhaps best introduced and explained in context. Therefore I have begun with information about some of the pioneering approaches to collaborating with nature, about healthy soil and biodiversity. The perennial vegetables are introduced and explained in the context of my experiments and how I have learned to grow in polycultures. This is real life and of course things did not always go according to plan; I have not hidden my mistakes as each one teaches something.

Both perennial vegetables and growing in polycultures are likely to be unfamiliar to many people; but they are well worth trying out and integrating into your garden too. You don't need much space, or time, or any particular expertise. As with any new endeavour you do need some patience and ideally becoming more sensitive to how nature works will really help.

I am thrilled with the results of my experiments with both perennial vegetables and polycultures. There are other perennial vegetables that are not included here as I have focussed particularly on those that I have had the best results with. I think that once you have the concept established and have some experience of growing polycultures that they can come in an almost infinite variety. Mine now include other more conventional vegetables that can be grown as virtual perennials, as well as wild flowers, herbs and fruit bushes.

In one sense this will never be a finished work but it has reached a point where there is sufficient information of interest and significance to seek to share with a wider audience. The techniques proposed here are not set in stone and just as I have experimented to find what works for me I hope that other gardeners will experiment with perennial vegetables and polycultures.

I hope that I have produced an interesting introduction to an as yet unfamiliar topic. Perennial vegetables deserve much more attention. They can provide reliable harvests through much of the year for little work, and when grown in polycultures according to natural principles they help build fertility and enrich local ecosystems. My hope is that you will be inspired to start experimenting too.

chapter 1

SETTING AN OBJECTIVE

To find and grow as many perennial vegetables as possible

Despite initial disappointment, the idea of perennial vegetables had so possessed me that I could not give up without finding out if my dream was possible.

Starting points

It is becoming clearer daily that we live in uncertain times. One aspect of this uncertainty is increasing food prices and I am therefore sure that I am not alone in feeling an instinct to grow at least some of my own food. I have long harboured a secret envy of those gardeners who can bring forth a bountiful harvest from a beautiful plot but my previous attempts to grow vegetables have been short lived, somewhat half hearted and less than successful. Loving gardening does not make me anything other than a very average gardener, either before I began this project or now, therefore anything I can do, anyone else can also do. I was probably first attracted to growing perennial vegetables because they sounded easy and trouble free; and by then experience had taught me that this was likely to be the only kind of food growing I might succeed with – if I could find out what to grow and where to get it from.

Happily perennial vegetables are sufficiently robust to withstand my less than refined horticultural skills and also the vagaries of my garden, which is hardly ideal for 'normal' vegetables any way. Once I had understood the theory I began to search for and experiment with perennial vegetables and out in the garden the polyculture patches are burgeoning with life! I have spent long hours on the internet searching out information, tracking down perennials, many of which were not available in the UK seven or eight years ago. I have had to acquire at least a modicum of competence in raising plants from seed, although some have defeated me every time. However once the polyculture patches became established things began to fall into place and whilst there has been both triumph and disaster I have found it an easy, enjoyable and labour saving way of growing food.

Be realistic but push the boundaries of possibility

Although I would have dearly loved to grow a large scale forest garden, I was of necessity, limited to the plot round the house. Most of the garden is in front of the house being approximately eleven metres by thirteen at its widest points. Most of this was and remains conventional lawn with shrubby edges and a number of small trees. The 'back' garden is actually to the side of the house and is smaller than the front. Figures 1, 2 and 3 show the position of the early polyculture patches within the garden as of 2011.

The first polyculture patch was a small bed in the back garden which started out measuring about two metres by three. For years it had been home to a rampant hazel tree, an outsized conifer and a monster berberis. In an attempt to tame things the conifer and berberis had been removed, the hazel substantially reduced and the area replanted with shrubs and ornamentals beside a new timber deck just three months before I learned about forest gardens and began to hatch other plans.

This felt incredibly frustrating and I began to sneak vegetables in amongst the shrubs. Before I tracked down some perennial vegetables to begin experimenting with, these were annuals. The slugs won hands down eating everything in sight. The shrubs I had chosen did not like the site either and most of them withered away and died. Over the coming couple of years as I began to locate perennial vegetables this unpromising start metamorphosed into a delightful polyculture. I did not really know what I was doing to start with and gradually I 'stole' more bits of the garden for polyculture experiments. It therefore developed in a very piecemeal fashion with the initial patch creeping out by degrees and a couple more patches started.

The second polyculture bed is in a shady corner in the back corner of the front garden measuring approximately five metres by four. Until autumn 2010 it had a goat willow in the corner (which no doubt took up a lot of fertility and water), plus an existing small apple tree at the back. Although it had been 'lawn' it is naturally so damp that grass would not actually grow over most of it and there was some other ground cover that I have never identified masquerading as grass. Bounded on one side by a fence and the neighbouring property and on another by a wall

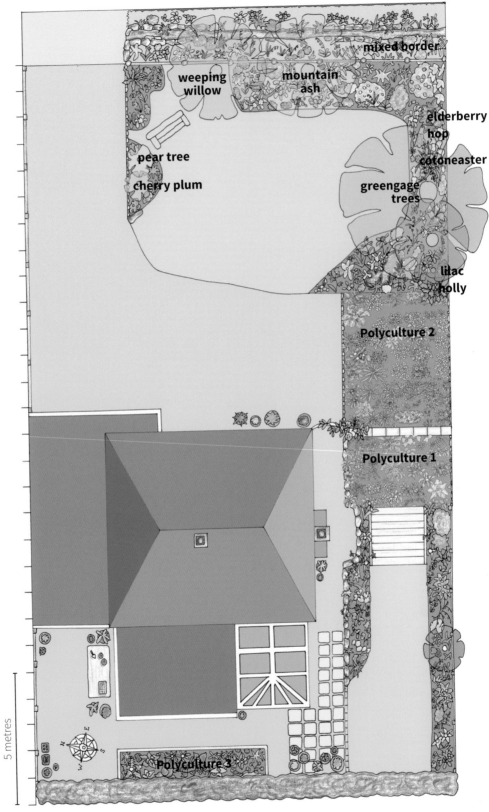

Figure 1: The whole garden showing the polyculture patches situated either side of the wall dividing the front and back gardens.

Figure 2: The first polyculture patch situated in the back garden and home to a diverse polyculture of perennial vegetables.

KEY

Figure 2: Back Garden
1   Climbing rose
2   Walking stick kale
3   Grape, grown from pip
4   Nepalese raspberry
5   Raspberry
6   Blackberry
7   Cherry tree
8   Miscellaneous kales
9   Yams
10 Blackcurrant
11 Fennel
12 Asparagus
13 Variegated Daubenton's kale
14 Field beans / broad beans
15 Groundnut
16 Clover
17 Welsh onion
18 Yacon
19 Nine star perennial broccoli
20 Wild beet
21 Wild leek
22 Spinach mediana
23 Asturian kale
24 Green Daubenton's kale
25 Hazel
26 Wild strawberry
27 Clove pink
28 Buckler leaf sorrel

29 Mixed onions, ground cover, rocky edge
30 Feverfew
31 Perennial leek
32 Chick pea
33 Sweet cicely
34 Tiger nut
35 Scorzonera
36 Oca
37 Buffalo currant

Figure 3: Front Garden
1   Field beans / broad beans
2   Oca
3   1,000 headed kale
4   Bronze fennel
5   Maximillian sunflower
6   Pink clover
7   Asturian kale
8   Stinging nettles
9   Nine star perennial broccoli
10 Earth nut pea
11 Groundnut
12 Jerusalem artichoke
13 Miscellaneous kales
14 Holly
15 *Ceanothus*
16 Mixed edge of ivy, wild strawberry, herb Robert, mints, honeysuckle, creeping Jenny, oxlip, *euonymus*,

wild raspberry, wild violet, *vinca*, wild garlic, hairy bittercress, foxglove three cornered leek
17 Purple sprouting broccoli
18 Wild rocket
19 Wild chicory
20 Land cress
21 Skirret
22 Yams
23 Chinese artichoke
24 Marjoram
25 Asphodel
26 Earth nut pea, French beans, shallot Chinese artichoke
27 Spinach
28 Red veined sorrel
29 Blackcurrant
30 Apple tree
31 Raspberry
32 Leeks
33 *Eleagnus*
34 Wild strawberry
35 Three cornered leek and wild garlic
36 Sweet cicely
37 *Pyracantha*
38 Gooseberry
     Inbetween plants are: dandelion, dead nettles, sweet woodruff, cleavers, herb Robert, self heal, bluebell, crocus, daffodil

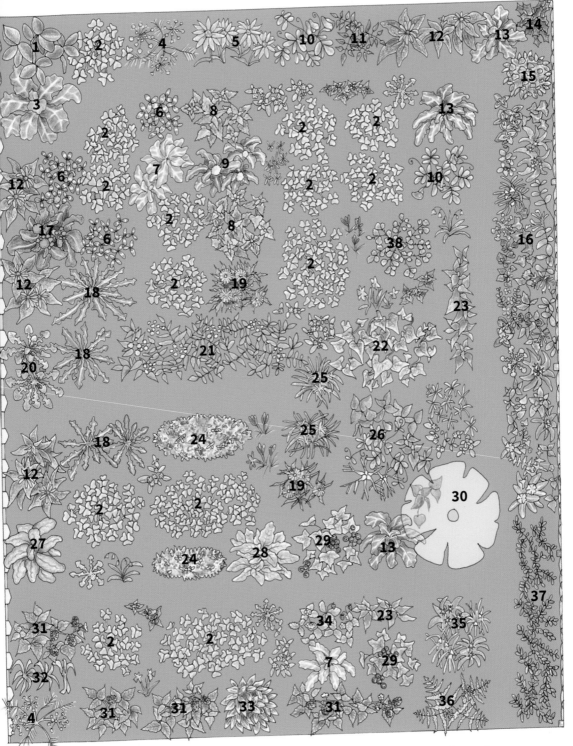

Figure 3: The second polyculture patch which is slightly larger but shadier and situated in the front garden.

The first polyculture patch is the area of green behind the decking (May 2011).

The second polyculture patch in the back corner of the front garden (May 2011).

A narrow strip at the back of the garden pressed into service as the third polyculture patch (May 2012).

separating front and back gardens, it is quite a shaded spot. Sunlight is mainly early in the morning or late evening during the summer and even then it is filtered through tall trees. It is not what would conventionally be thought of as a vegetable plot, but I was desperate!

The third bed is a short narrow strip no more than a metre wide behind the kitchen window bordered by an old established privet hedge. Other parts of the garden have also been pressed into service. Random vegetables have appeared in flower beds and in odd shady corners. Some have worked out others not, but often the outcome has been opposite to my initial expectations. I have found polycultures are quite addictive and in spring last year the back lawn was taken up to make more room for growing.

Clearly there is scope to plant polycultures almost anywhere – in a very small space or equally to expand to fill a very large space. Anyone sadly living without a garden or access to land can grow them in pots, though it is harder to meet their requirements for adequate nutrients and water in such confined spaces. Details of some 'potted polycultures' are given in Chapter Ten. I have also attempted to push the boundaries by experimenting by growing 'normal' annual vegetables as perennials (see Chapter Six).

Definitions

Most gardeners are familiar with the terms describing habits and life histories of plants but for anyone who is not here is a quick outline. Annual plants flower and set seed in their first season, then they die. Most food plants the world over are annuals, but this was not always the case. Biennial plants flower and set seed in their second season. Some food plants are biennials but are used in their first year. Carrots, beetroot, swede and parsnip fall into this category making them effectively annuals.

In contrast perennials live on for more than two years. Local conditions of climate, soil and seasons determine where specific perennials will grow well. Apart from fruit trees and bushes very few of our main food plants are perennial, asparagus and globe artichoke being perhaps two of the best known perennial vegetables.

What is special about perennial vegetables?

- Perennial vegetables are reliable performers and producers. Obviously they are not totally indestructible, but their proven durability is reassuring and once established they can last for years.

- Once established they need little care compared to annual vegetables.

- Very little (if any) physical labour is required to establish and maintain them in a polyculture, making them eminently suitable for anyone with little time or energy.

- Some perennial vegetables are wild vegetables or have not moved far from their wild origins. They are often resilient and adaptable plants and can be grown on land that annual vegetables would despise. Many of mine are, of necessity, growing in semi shade and some are in total shade. They have enabled me to make the best of the conditions I have and for that I am eternally grateful.

- I have had no need for any fancy gadgets and gizmos beloved of some gardening magazines and colour supplements.

- Perennial vegetables are mainly productive during the spring and autumn and to some extent the winter. There is something of a lull in the warmer summer months. This gap provides an opportunity for including any summer favourites amongst the perennials or tending to a conventional vegetable patch during that time, or safely going on holiday without fearing the perennial vegetables are in mortal danger.

- Plants that remain in situ through the year contribute to soil fertility through the 'live food web' whereas the bare soil of an annual vegetable patch can lose fertility (see Chapter Three).

- A diversity of plant heights and shapes helps support increased biodiversity.

- During the course of experimenting with perennial vegetables and writing this book we seem to have experienced a series of extreme weather events – in Shropshire where I live we have had several extremely wet, cool, dull summers from 2007 to 2009; two very severe winters – 2009-2010 and 2010-2011; a very dry summer in 2011 followed by a very, very wet one in 2012 and then a record breaking period of snow and extreme cold in spring 2013. Such changeability makes any form of gardening challenging but overall the perennial vegetables have held on remarkably well. It would not be realistic to expect everything to cope with every extreme of weather and there have been some casualties such as the kale that not surprisingly froze to death nearly totally encased in frozen snow for weeks last winter.

- Nobody can predict with any certainty the precise way that climate change will impact on weather over the coming years, but if we are to experience increased diversity and extremes perhaps having an increased diversity of food plants growing in our gardens is one way to help mitigate the impact.

- Growing perennials in polycultures brings additional benefits which are described in later chapters.

I would never claim that perennial vegetables are a replacement for annual vegetables but I am sure they have a significant role to play in the food growing of the future. They are not show stopping celebrities but reliable performers that are immensely rewarding to grow and eat.

Are there any disadvantages?

- At present some perennial vegetable seeds are undoubtedly more expensive than those of their annual cousins. Sometimes seeds are a one-off expense as some species can be propagated from saved seed.

- Perennial vegetables are not often obtainable through the major seed and nursery suppliers. However even though some of my plants and seeds have been obtained from Europe this is not difficult to do and Appendix Two gives details of the suppliers I have used. I am quite pleased that perennial vegetables are a niche in the horticultural market not filled by big corporations and much prefer to buy from small, independent companies.

- Cool temperate climates (as in Britain) do not support perennial fruiting or podding vegetables. If you want to grow things like perennial beans or gourds and squashes you will need to move to somewhere suitable like California or Hawaii.

Find and grow as many perennial vegetables as possible

Selecting the best perennials for your own circumstances may take some trial and error. My initial experiments began with plants such as Good King Henry, lovage and salad burnet. I did not like any of these and nearly gave up at this point. I don't want to malign them though, they have their place – as in a forest garden where there is plenty of room for them – and where they undoubtedly bring a host of benefits, and some people may well like them. Despite initial disappointment the idea of perennial vegetables had so possessed me that I could not give up without finding out if my dream was possible. I continued searching for perennials that would work for me and decided to track down seeds or plants of every variety I possibly could to see if they would grow in my garden and what they tasted like.

Eventually this ambition meant that I was almost overwhelmed with a host of different plants to experiment with. There were seedlings everywhere and young plants bursting out of pots with no designated place to live in the vegetable patch. I found out what I should have anticipated from the outset – that my lack of skills and experience caused a good deal of failures. Growing a lot of new plants, all of which were precious, in a very limited space and fitting this in between work and all the other demands on time has been challenging. Some plants inevitably did not get

Pots and seedlings galore in the spring sunshine (April 2011).

the care they needed and deserved; and I have not yet been able to try absolutely all the plants that I would have liked. But at least this is a reflection of real life and the really exciting thing is that despite these disadvantages it works!

I am completely indebted to Ken Fern and his Plants for a Future database.[*] Without this monumental reference I would not have been able to even begin the background research (other books and websites that have useful information about perennial vegetables are listed in Appendix Three). At the latest count I have experimented with somewhere in the region of sixty perennial or potentially perennial vegetables. My experiments will no doubt continue but for the purposes of collecting things together for this book I have identified the perennial vegetables that I have found to be most useful.

Although many perennial vegetables are robust and reasonably easy to grow, some species require more care in the sowing and / or establishment and some have narrower tolerances for soil pH, light and water than others. The perennial vegetables I am recommending have been successfully and happily grown in my polycultures. I hope these conditions are sufficiently representative of conditions pertaining in many gardens in the UK and that therefore they might realistically be expected to thrive across most parts of the UK and also similar cool, temperate climates in other parts of the world. Those that I tried that did not produce good results are detailed in Chapter Six as they may well fare better in different soils and with drier and sunnier locations than I can provide.

Principles

I started with perennial vegetables simply hoping to find easy ways of growing food. Over time this aim has matured and ultimately evolved into an absorbing project and this book. It took time to fully unfold what was needed and could be achieved, but with some hindsight I can now define a set of core guiding principles and aims.

Conserve energy

It is estimated[†] that about **10 times** more energy is needed to produce food in what has become the conventional fashion than is realised by eating it. Surely for any

[*] www.pfaf.org/user/default.aspx
[†] Soule and Piper 1992, quoted in *Edible Forest Gardens – ecological vision and theory for temperate climate permaculture, Volume One: Vision and Theory*; David Jacke with Eric Toensmeier, Chelsea Green Publishing Company, Vermont, 2005 page 23

form of food growing or production to have a chance of being sustainable in the long term it must drastically improve on this horrifying statistic.

I have borne in mind the calorific value of the vegetables I grow, or more often the likely value, as many are not included in standard nutritional tables. Leafy green vegetables are low in calories therefore it makes no sense to me to spend physical effort producing them. Ideally they need to be available to just pick off the plant on a more or less permanent basis and perennial greens fit this very well. More calories are potentially derived from roots and tubers that are energy stores for the plant, although some like Jerusalem artichokes are stores of sugars that are not digestible and therefore their calories are not available. Either way, the less energy put in to the garden the better, you have more time, nature gets to do more of the work, energy is saved going shopping and less needs to be grown within a system that is frankly mad.

As a consequence my first aim is **to use as little energy as possible**. As an organic gardener anyway this clearly includes not using artificial inputs like fertilisers and pesticides, **but equally I wanted to put as little personal physical effort in as possible**.

Nurture and cherish a healthy and fertile soil

Soil is an immensely precious resource. I am in awe of this darkened realm which ultimately supports all life on the planet. This was not something I knew or understood to begin with; following natural principles for supporting soil health is fundamental to my gardening whether it be for vegetables or flowers and shrubs.

Conserve water and moisture

I water seedlings until they are planted out and established. Otherwise watering only happens under exceptional circumstances – after long periods without rain and when plants are starting to wilt. In practice it has only been during the unusually dry summer of 2011 that I have had to regularly water the polycultures and even then it was only the green vegetables in sunny places that needed it. High volumes of organic matter have built up in the soil helping to retain moisture, as does mulch on the soil surface and for the most part this keeps the polyculture beds sufficiently damp through normal dry spells.

Grow polycultures

The theory and practice of polycultures is covered in Chapters Four, Eight, Nine, Ten and Eleven. Environmentally and ecologically this way of growing is extraordinarily beneficial. It provides diverse habitat niches which nature fills with networks of life which in turn contributes to the overall health and fertility of the patch and the surrounding environment.

A polyculture can potentially be as orderly or as random as the individual gardener wants. As long as the plants are happy, the actual layout can be an approximation of something neat like a potager or much wilder and freer, either way can be very visually attractive.

Follow and celebrate nature

All the above principles can be summed up as following and celebrating nature. Nature is efficient; she conserves energy and produces no waste. She constructs complex webs of life that boost fertility and promote variety and diversity in unplanned but endlessly beautiful and productive ways. Much of what follows is about unwrapping and applying that principle.

Forest garden.
Photo: Martin Crawford
The Agroforestry Research Trust
Forest Garden Project

chapter 2

FOUNDATIONS AND UNDERLYING THEMES
Permaculture, forest gardening and natural farming

Forest gardening, permaculture and natural farming are all ideas whose time has definitely come. They have been originated and developed by people of insight and foresight, who decades ago looked towards our current day and foresaw the need to do things differently. The rest of the world is beginning to catch on to this need, but there is a lot of catching up to do. It is not sufficient to leave this to politicians, policy makers, business or other people in general; we all need to be involved and we all can be! This exploration of these three fascinating topics is a tour of the work of some amazingly inspirational and dedicated pioneers.

Permaculture

In a drive for economic and material wealth and security, humanity has created global systems of waste and destruction with scant regard for the consequences. As a result spoiled landscapes, damaged ecosystems, extinct or endangered plants and animals, wasted resources, waste materials, holes in the ozone layer, melting polar ice caps, stockpiled weapons, unhealthy populations consuming food that has been stripped of its nutritional value, have all become commonplace in industrialised societies the world over. Faced with such overwhelming problems it is easy to feel powerless to make a difference. I am sure many people prefer to avoid dwelling on environmental and ecological problems because of the profound discomfort this can engender when faced with one's own personally limited sphere of influence.

This is where permaculture fits in. It is modelled on the principles of nature and natural systems which do not waste and despoil and encompasses philosophy, values and practical strategies for action. Initially it focussed on land based activities (gardening and farming) but its principles of 'Earth care', 'fair shares' and 'people care' are clearly very widely applicable. Thus it also encompasses design of the wider built environment and elements within it. Its broad approach uses new methods and practices derived from many disciplines formulated to solve specific problems alongside older techniques that have been largely abandoned. It therefore provides a framework for addressing the basic human needs of food, energy, shelter and a whole host of 21st century dilemmas by adopting its principles for practical solutions that provide safeguards against unwise and damaging actions. There are many ingenious people out there doing all sorts of fascinating things the importance of which cannot be underestimated.

I am not trained in permaculture but have naturally absorbed the essence of it through the experience of growing in polycultures. Appendix Three gives details of interesting books, publications and web sites for further information.

Edible forest gardening

Edible forest gardening is one aspect of a permaculture approach to growing food. Variations on the forest gardening theme occur (or occurred) in traditional cultures around the globe. However 'development' and the importation of European / western agricultural practices have largely displaced the old ways. With its roots deep in ancient practices, forest gardening is being rediscovered by the 'developed' world as a remarkably useful and relevant approach to growing food.

On Wenlock Edge in Shropshire, a handful of miles from my home, the late Robert Hart created a prototype forest garden. He was a man of insight and also a practical man trying to work out how to grow food for himself and his brother in as easy and efficient way as he could. Instead of opting for intensive production techniques, he decided to model nature and this led him to the concept he articulated and wrote about as 'forest gardening'.

The vegetation in a forest garden is usually described in terms of distinct layers. At the top the tallest trees form a canopy with smaller trees and shrubs beneath; still lower are the medium height herbaceous plants and low ground covers. A final 'layer' of climbers and vines mingle amongst all the layers from the ground upwards. The forest garden therefore has enormous variety in height and physical form. This in turn translates into ecological diversity by providing living quarters or niches for an extraordinarily wide range of animal and insect life. Nature has a marvellous ability to take a set of parts and knit them together into a system which is eventually capable of meeting its own needs.

One feature of such a system is that it is far less susceptible to pests and diseases. There is a long food chain within the system and natural predators abound. This helps to prevent pests from building up to threatening levels. It is also likely that individual trees and plants are healthy in themselves which either deters pests or enables diseases to be countered more effectively. By contrast a monoculture, whether it be forest or farm is readily susceptible to pests and diseases due to the high number of a single species in a small area and lack of diversity in natural predators.

Sunlight is the essential energy from which all other energy on the planet is ultimately derived. The layering of space in a forest garden enables it to capture the maximum amount of sunlight and convert this into plant biomass. Temperate forests are known to be ecosystems that generate a high level of plant biomass anyway and the really clever thing about forest gardens is that by using as many edible plants as possible a high proportion of this biomass is actually food. Additionally a well designed forest garden should continue to increase in productivity over time and needs less maintenance and work than a comparable area under conventional forestry or farming.

It is unlikely that any single variety grown in a forest garden will produce as much food as it might under more intensive systems. However the total output of all the edible species combined is greater than could be produced from the same plot of land under conventional cultivation. This is known as the principle of additional yields.

Forest gardens are shady places but they are in no way dull, gloomy or dark. Spacing trees more widely than in conventional woodlands leave openings in the tree canopy and the overall impression is light and airy rather than dark and dank. Plenty of trees, shrubs and herbaceous plants are well able to thrive whilst living in a degree of shade, and larger open spaces can be left for plants which really need full sun. The design can bring out wonderful contrasts between the different elements of the garden and it starts to feel a magical and beautiful place.

Other pioneers have now picked up where Robert Hart was obliged to leave this story. Martin Crawford is Director of the Agroforestry Research Trust based at Dartington in the beautiful South Hams area of south Devon. His experimental forest garden, created in the grounds of Dartington Hall is a wonder and Martin is a phenomenon. His attention to detail and the range of his experimentation and research has vastly increased the knowledge that is now available on forest gardening. Martin's book on *Creating A Forest Garden*[*] is certain to become a classic reference for UK forest

[*] *Creating a Forest Garden – working with nature to grow edible crops*; Martin Crawford; Green Books; Dartington, 2010

gardeners and permaculturists. I attended an inspirational course with him in 2006 and am in awe of his lovely garden and extraordinary knowledge.

Meanwhile, across the Atlantic, Dave Jacke and Eric Toensmeier have written a two volume book on edible forest gardens. The context is North American, although they feature the UK forest gardens created by Robert Hart and Martin Crawford, both of which they have visited. They too have brought an incredible wealth of knowledge together in their two volumes on how to make an edible forest garden. I have been reading and rereading these since they were published and will probably always mine them for deeper understanding and more ideas. If you have an appetite for further study and meticulous detail about the science of ecosystems, soil and many related topics then this must be on your reading and rereading list.

In addition to producing diverse edible crops, forest gardens can be planted with a range of trees, shrubs and herbaceous plants to fulfil other functions. Examples include bamboo which is edible but also used for garden canes, coppiced hazel for fuel, charcoal and a range of garden products, other plants for dyes, medicinal herbs and other uses.

Forest gardening sounds almost too good to be true, but there is no hidden catch to the theory or practice. Although I think that a thorough understanding of the principles and science behind it, and careful planning and preparation are essential keys to success. But forest gardening is truly amazing, and a potential answer to the problem of how to achieve high yields of food from small areas with minimal inputs. It is eminently suited to individuals raising food from their own plots, rather than the vast acreages of corporate agriculture and its potential significance cannot be overstated.

Masanobu Fukuoka and natural farming

Masanobu Fukuoka is another hero of mine and I cannot pay sufficient tribute to his life and work. He was truly inspired. His life, work and overall approach has been a significant influence and has helped me apply the practices and principles of permaculture and forest gardening to growing perennial vegetables in polycultures.

Masanobu Fukuoka lived and died in rural Japan between 1913 and 2008. Initially he studied plant pathology and worked as a produce inspector for the local customs

---

* *Edible Forest Gardens – ecological vision and theory for temperate climate permaculture, Volume One: Vision and Theory; Volume Two: Design and Practice*; David Jacke with Eric Toensmeier; Chelsea Green Publishing Company, Vermont, 2005

office. Following a period of ill health and depression a profound experience brought him to a new way of perceiving and interacting with the world. He describes this life changing event and his feelings of elation:

"My spirit became light and clear. I was dancing wildly for joy. I could hear the small birds chirping in the trees, and see the distant waves glistening in the rising sun. The leaves danced clear and sparkling. I felt that this was truly heaven on earth. Everything that had possessed me, all the agonies, disappeared like dreams and illusions, and something one might call 'true nature' stood revealed."

This event marked a complete turning point in his life. He was convinced that he had gained an important insight which was potentially of great benefit to many people. Unsure at first about how to communicate it to other people he decided to return to the family farm and demonstrate his new perception in a highly practical and visible way by applying it to farming. It was this quest that eventually led him to the timeless principles of what he termed 'natural farming':

• No cultivation...
• No chemical fertiliser or prepared compost...
• No weeding by tillage or herbicides...
• No dependence on chemicals..."[†]

Natural farming is fundamentally about these core principles; it does not and never could provide a detailed method. Fukuoka recounts in his book *The One-Straw Revolution* how he came in time to develop a method of cultivating (or not cultivating), the local crops of rice and barley. He did this by what he called 'do nothing' farming which he describes thus:

"I was aiming at a pleasant, natural way of farming which results in making the work easier instead of harder. 'How about not doing this? How about not doing that?' – that was my way of thinking. I ultimately reached the conclusion that there was no need to plough, no need to apply fertiliser, no need to make compost, no need to use insecticide. When you get right down to it, there are few agricultural practices that are really necessary."[‡]

His conclusion was that interference with nature inevitably unbalances it and the ideal was to interfere as little as possible. However on the journey to that conclusion

* *The One-Straw Revolution*; Masanobu Fukuoka; New York, 2009; pp.8-9
† *The One-Straw Revolution*; Masanobu Fukuoka; New York, 2009
‡ *The One-Straw Revolution*; Masanobu Fukuoka; New York, 2009

he made some truly disastrous mistakes. Leaving productive orchards unpruned the branches became tangled, the trees were savagely attacked by insects and died. As he sought the answer to the question, "what is the natural pattern?", he killed hundreds more trees before finally understanding what a completely natural fruit tree was like. It is testament to the certainty of his commitment to natural principles that he was prepared to endure such losses and yet persist in the search.

Fukuoka persisted with his experiments for decades, using orchard fruit, rice, barley and vegetables. In time he was able to raise crops with yields equal to or exceeding the average for an industrialised farm in his region without any of the intrusive techniques and additional inputs. Word spread and many enthusiasts came to live a very simple life on the mountain above the farm and to learn by working on the farm how Fukuoka worked.

Despite Japanese government agriculture department officials being well aware of his success no attempt was ever made by officials to spread his methods amongst other farmers. His important work and contribution to understanding nature has become widely recognised, however, and *The One-Straw Revolution* is now widely regarded as a classic work.

Synthesis

Copying nature seems to me to be a very practical proposition - after all what might we know that she does not? The visionaries of permaculture, forest gardening and natural farming have all wisely and cleverly adopted and adapted natural principles and I have aimed to follow in their footsteps. Permaculture principles underpin my aims, forest gardening has provided essential techniques whilst natural farming inspires me to follow nature as closely as possible.

A wider context

Clearly the wider context of any action we take is significant. I have placed my experiments with perennial vegetables in the context of permaculture, forest gardening and natural farming because I could not have done it without them. However I think it is necessary to put all of these within a yet wider context – that of transition.

The Transition Movement was launched in 2006 in Totnes, Devon and rapidly spread round the world. The purpose in their own words is:

What are we 'transitioning' towards?

Whether we like it or not, over the next decade or two, we'll be transitioning to a lower energy future - essential because of climate change and inevitable because of diminishing supplies of fossil fuels (particularly oil).

There are a variety of possible outcomes depending on whether we stick our heads in the sand or whether we start working for a future that we want.

Transition Initiatives, community by community, are actively and cooperatively creating happier, fairer and stronger communities, places that work for the people living in them and are far better suited to dealing with the shocks that'll accompany our economic and energy challenges and a climate in chaos.

It begins when a small group comes together with a shared concern about shrinking supplies of cheap energy (peak oil), climate change and increasingly, economic downturn. This group recognises that:

- Climate change and peak oil require urgent action.
- Life with less energy is inevitable. It is better to plan for it than to be taken by surprise.
- Industrial society has lost the resilience to be able to cope with energy shocks.
- We have to act together, now.
- Infinite growth within a finite system (such as planet Earth) is impossible.
- We demonstrated great ingenuity and intelligence as we raced up the energy curve over the last 150 years. There's no reason why we can't use those qualities, and more, as we negotiate our way up from the depths back towards the sun and air.

If we plan and act early enough, and use our creativity and cooperation to unleash the genius within our local communities, we can build a future far more fulfilling and en-riching, more connected to and more gentle on the Earth, than the life we have today.'

Transition was born out of permaculture design and encompasses every aspect of life, but one core theme, because it is utterly essential, is food production. The approach of many transitioners to food growing is rooted in natural principles. If you have not heard about transition please look at their website and follow links to the many incredibly positive and ingenious things that are happening. Local groups have projects such as garden share schemes, community gardens, forest gardens, foraging walks and workshops, community supported agriculture, all of which are positive moves to a more secure future.

· www.transitionnetwork.org/support/what-transition-initiative, as of 26 November 2011

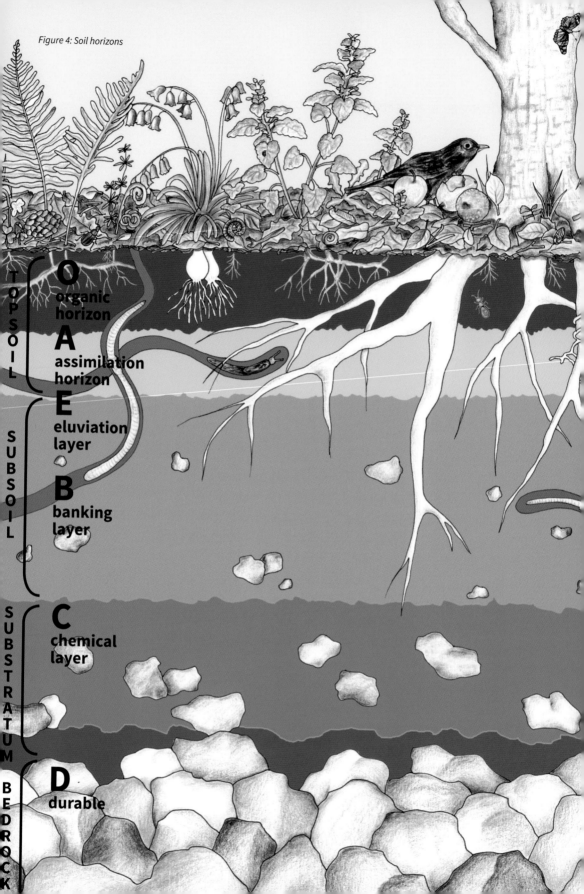

Figure 4: Soil horizons

T O P S O I L

O organic horizon

A assimilation horizon

S U B S O I L

E eluviation layer

B banking layer

S U B S T R A T U M

C chemical layer

B E D R O C K

D durable

chapter 3

LIVING SOIL AND PLANT NUTRITION

Soil is complex, fascinating and utterly fundamental to all life.
It is therefore essential to have some understanding of how to
support and maintain a vibrant, living soil.

When I was a child the word 'soil' was absent from my vocabulary. Instead I learned the words 'dirt' and 'earth' and as a child was frequently reminded that 'dirt' was to be avoided at all costs in order to keep myself and my clothes clean. But even then I must have had a fascination with soil and I enjoyed digging it up surreptitiously and making the outlawed 'mud pies' (muddy versions of sand castles) in a bucket behind the garden shed. When eventually I had my first garden I could not get out into it fast enough to plunge my hands into the soil. Now that I know a bit more about what soil is and how it functions I am in ever increasing awe of it.

To grow anything, I think it helps to understand something of how soil is structured and the soil life that brings with it health and fertility. To grow perennial polycultures I think it is even more useful as the very fact of their perennial nature means that life is persistently present and that brings its own benefits as described below.

The basics of soil structure

Soil structure is generally described in terms of horizontal layers or 'horizons' (*see Figure 4*). In a natural undisturbed soil the uppermost layer is composed of freshly deposited and partly decomposed vegetation and known as the 'organic horizon'. This is often removed by gardeners for the sake of neatness and presentation and also it is often believed to avoid plant disease. However if left in situ it will absorb rainfall and hold onto moisture, protect from erosion and compaction and make a cosy layer of insulation moderating the temperature beneath. It also provides a home for insects and removing it can favour unwanted fungi, bacteria and insects.

Below this is the 'assimilation horizon'. Hopefully, if it has had the benefit of organic matter added from above it will be rich in humus which is the end product of decayed organic matter. This is a stable form of organic matter, taken below ground level by the action of worms and other soil creatures. It holds nutrients but makes them available to plant roots, increases air and water retention and enables better aggregation of soil particles. Humus rich soil has a characteristic dark brown colour.

The next layer down is the 'eluviation layer', a relatively lifeless band with limited storage capacity for nutrients. Those nutrients not held in any form of living or dead organic matter are washed downwards through this layer by the movement of water.

The 'banking layer' beneath is where minerals are able to collect themselves together again by forming mineral clays. However for these to be available for plant growth a deep rooted plant or tree has to tap into them or alternatively worms can also retrieve nutrients and bring them up higher in the soil.

Deeper still are the realms of mineral particles and bed rock, but which are not home to any life.

I continuously add material to the top layer of my polyculture patches. I cut back or pull out plants ('weeds') which are getting a bit big and just drop them where I stand. I mulch round larger plants like oca with cut up material from shrubs, nettles, ferns, even twigs and small branches from elsewhere in the garden. The aim is everything being fed back to the soil with the absolute minimum of work. It is really quite surprising how much material the soil can take back, but I now confidently do this with everything that I would once have added to the compost heap.

Healthy soil is alive

Obviously I can't see the microscopic creatures that live in the soil, but on my travels through the garden I do see lots of evidence of worms, spiders, beetles, ladybirds, wood lice, flying creatures of all types, scuttling millipedes or centipedes and the birds that come to feed here seem to agree there is plenty to eat. These represent some of the creatures at the top of a largely invisible food chain.

Vast numbers of microscopic forms of animal life, fungi and bacteria live in healthy soil. Many of these are decomposers which break down lifeless organic matter (of plant or animal origin) and which in turn at the end of their lives become either a meal for another creature or part of the matter to be decomposed (*see Figure 5*).

Each of the organisms below is a store for nutrients during their life; after their death the nutrients become available to other life forms. Hence there are plenty of opportunities to retain and recycle nutrients through 'primary', 'secondary' and 'tertiary decomposers' in soils with strong and diverse populations.

Bacteria tend to feed on fresh organic matter or the exudates squeezed from plant roots

- They mostly decompose fresh organic matter though some strains work on more resistant organic debris.
- Many can decompose toxic organic chemicals.
- By their combined activities they store, release and recycle nutrients and secrete glues that bind soil particles together.
- The majority are beneficial organisms.

Soil fungi are mostly microscopic threadlike organisms

- They improve nutrient retention and recycling, soil texture and promote soil health.
- They are adapted to many different conditions and can live in and around plant roots, the litter layer, spaces in the soil and on organic matter.
- They function as decomposers and can work in association with plants to their mutual benefit by taking nutrients and transporting them long distances to feed them to plant roots.
- Some kill nematodes (and vice versa), some feed on insects and some suppress their disease causing cousins.
- Many can digest toxic organic chemicals.
- Decomposer fungi can digest woody substances and some attack sick or dying trees but do not touch healthy plants.
- Fungi store and transport both water and calcium.

Protozoa

- Are the simplest form of single celled soil animal life.

- They eat bacteria (good and bad) and some eat other protozoa.

Nematodes

- Eat fungi, bacteria, roots and other organisms.
- Some nematodes have earned the rest a bad name as causes of disease. Approximately 90% are beneficial and some species predate on the malign 10%.

Arthropods are the real creepy crawlies and include insects, spiders, mites, bugs, millipedes, centipedes living in tiny spaces between soil particles or in the litter layer

- Mites eat bacteria and fungi, shred organic matter and a few attack plants.
- Bugs, millipedes, beetles, ants, earwigs and insect larvae shred and start the decomposition of organic matter.
- Beetles, centipedes and spiders are predators controlling populations of other organisms.

Earthworms shred and eat organic matter, deriving much of their nourishment from the organisms that live on these materials

- Their smaller cousins, potworms, are general decomposers and grazers.
- All worms bury and shred plant residues, stimulate microbial activity, mix and aggregate soil, increase water holding capacity and provide channels for root growth.

The Soil Life Cycle

DO NOT DISTURB

Fung

Nutrients Released

Primary

Figure 5: The interdependence of life above and below ground as nutrients cycle continuously through the ecosystem.

Birds

Animals

Organic Matter

Arthropods

Bacteria

Mites

Protozoa

Earthworms

Nematodes

ers   Secondary Decomposers   Higher Level Decomposers

Soil food webs

It is the concept of a web of life in the soil that has stuck firmly in my mind and imagination and has helped me understand how to help the soil become and remain healthy and fertile. It has become a very important consideration that guides everything I do (and don't do) in the garden. It also helps to integrate understanding of soil structure and soil life as twin aspects of the same system. I first learned about this concept from Jacke and Toensmeier.[*] To fully appreciate the complexity of these living systems please read their full account in their book, *Edible Forest Gardens*.

At any one time the nutrients used by plants may be stored in a variety of places – in bedrock, soil mineral particles, soil water, dead soil organic matter, soil organisms, live plants and the atmosphere. There are a variety of mechanisms by which nutrients are conserved and cycled within the soil or unfortunately lost.

A lifeless soil comprises only mineral particles, water and air. Nutrients can only be acquired from bedrock (very, very slowly), mineral particles or from the atmosphere. When it rains many of the available nutrients are quickly leached down to the sub soil and lost. There is no food for any soil organisms and the soil is essentially dead.

Dead food web

If anything that once lived is added to the soil the process of decomposition begins and a niche is created for a range of decomposer organisms. The life, work and interactions of these organisms can be thought of as the 'dead food web'. However eventually the process will be complete and if no further dead matter is added those organisms die. Humus has been added and temporarily provides a source of additional nutrients but eventually these will be leached out by rainfall.

Living food web

Part of the magic of plants is that when they are introduced to a dead system they initiate a range of functions and interactions that transform it into a living and life giving system.

[*] *Edible Forest Gardens – ecological vision and theory for temperate climate permaculture, Volume One: Vision and Theory*; David Jacke with Eric Toensmeier; Chelsea Green Publishing Company, Vermont, 2005

In a soil bursting with plants:

- They garner the sun's energy to grow and in effect they store embodied sunshine in their tissues. This is the starting point and channel for the energy that powers the 'system'; energy that is transferred to all the other life forms that feed on plants or on those animals which initially fed on plants and so on.

- They also hold nutrients in their tissues. Eventually dead plant tissue feeds the soil based decomposer organisms and breaks down into humus.

- Their roots extract nutrients from soil water preventing them being leached and lost.

- Secretions from plant roots feed soil microbes encouraging the growth of bacterial and fungal populations in the root zone.

- In return soil organisms facilitate the direct uptake of nutrients from organic and mineral matter.

This is a lively dynamic system – a live food web which will not come to an end while the sun still shines and the plants remain in situ. However if plants are removed, as for example in an annual vegetable patch, the life giving processes are interrupted and the health of the whole system begins to be affected.

Plants need the right nutrients

Most plant tissue is built from commonly occurring elements – hydrogen, oxygen and carbon. In addition they also require nitrogen, phosphorus and sulphur and a range of minerals.* Limitation or deficiency of any of these can hamper growth and make plants more susceptible to disease. Nitrogen, phosphorus and sulphur tend to occur in old, decomposed organic matter whilst minerals can be held in the topsoil in association with humus.

The gardener's part

My aim is to grow perennial vegetables and polycultures in a way that is as far towards the natural end of the spectrum as possible and to shun taking control.

* The main minerals essential for plants are magnesium, potassium and calcium; whilst very small quantities of iron, boron, zinc, copper, selenium, manganese, silicon and molybdenum are also needed. These same nutrients are also vital to human health and nutrition and some examples of how they are used are given in Appendix 5.

Perennial plantings inherently provide stability and support increasing diversity and numbers of soil organisms which in turn ultimately improves soil health and fertility. The aim is that this fertility and diversity continues to build over time and my experience is that the polycultures have exhibited ever more vigorous and healthy plants year after year.

I try to keep my interventions to a minimum as they generally tend to damage and destroy the soil food web. Therefore:

- Retain a permanently planted layer at all times, using ground covers between larger plants. I would rather allow a few uninvited guests (weeds) to live a while (in effect acting as a green manure) than leave exposed soil.

- Allow plant material to accumulate on the soil to maintain a permanent litter layer covering the soil surface.

- To seek and absorb vital minerals from the soil and subsoil and concentrate these in plant tissues use deep rooted mineral accumulator plants such as comfrey, dandelion (yes I did say that), and wild chicory.

- To absorb atmospheric nitrogen (for use by bacteria living symbiotically on the root system) plant leguminous plants such as clover and alfalfa, or use annual beans – broad / runner / French or wild plants such as vetches.

- Apart from gently planting new plants and equally gently removing root vegetables do not dig – it kills soil organisms.

- Do not add chemical fertilisers – they kill soil organisms.

- Do not walk on the soil, keep to pathways – compaction drives air out.

- Build up the depth of soil over time – as more mulch material is added to the top this will naturally happen. My observation is that plants are increasingly productive as the soil becomes deeper.

Even though I realise that I have always loved soil, I now understand much more about it. That understanding plus experience of its bounty leads naturally to treating it with even greater care and respect. More about how this manifests in practical terms is discussed in Chapter Eleven on how I manage a polyculture.

It also seems important to note that I hope to avoid a utilitarian attitude that sees looking after the soil purely as a means to looking after our own best interests. It is surely indicative of the intrinsic wisdom of ancient traditions such as Traditional

Chinese Medicine and Ayurveda that they recognise Earth as an element* which must be kept in vital balance with all other elements. Imbalance ultimately leads to dysfunction and disease; perhaps gaining a similar perspective will enable us all to have a deeper reverence for the ground from which we all ultimately spring.

* Traditional Chinese Medicine recognises the five fundamental elements of fire, earth, metal, water and wood; Ayurvedic Medicine recognises space, air, fire, water and earth

Wild chicory powering skywards (June).

chapter 4

GROWING IN POLYCULTURES
Diversity by Design

Great power lies in the choice of plants – a carefully selected polyculture is a team that can effectively share the available resources to the maximum benefit of all its' members.

What is a polyculture?

Polyculture is not a buzzword. At its simplest it means more than one plant growing or being cultivated together. Diversity is not just interesting and fun, it is essential to health and fertility and a well balanced polyculture is a team that shares the available resources to the advantage of the whole team.

In addition to a collection of perennial vegetables my garden is full of plants that serve specific purposes. Some keep pests at bay, others pull minerals from the subsoil or fix nitrogen from the air, keep the ground covered and feed bees and other insects. The ecological term for a natural assembly of plants that fulfils a complete set of requirements is a guild. It follows that all guilds will be polycultures, but not all polycultures will be guilds. Jacke and Toensmeier* give an excellent and readable explanation of the relevant ecological science.

* *Edible Forest Gardens – ecological vision and theory for temperate climate permaculture, Volume One: Vision and Theory*; David Jacke with Eric Toensmeier; Chelsea Green Publishing Company, Vermont, 2005

The advantages of polycultures

Annual vegetables make heavy demands on soil fertility whereas growing perennials in a polyculture seems to help boost increase soil fertility. A healthy polyculture will have links to its surrounding environment, bringing in birds, insects and other life and establishing a two way benefit.

As with soils the science behind ecological guilds is complex but thankfully it is not essential to understand its intricacies to create an effective polyculture. The following elements are all necessary and further details on choosing and siting the right plants for different purposes are given in Chapter Nine.

The elements of polycultures

Mineral accumulators

Mineral accumulators are plants that store vital minerals in their tissues at particularly high concentrations. Often this is done via a deep tap root which garners nutrients from the sub soil. Well known mineral accumulators include comfrey, nettles, dandelion and chicory.

Nitrogen fixers

Nitrogen fixing plants, which are mainly in the pea and bean family, take nitrogen from the air and incorporate it into their tissues. In a forest garden you would usually look for perennial nitrogen fixers, which can include a variety of shrubs. However at the scale of a perennial vegetable polyculture it can sometimes be more useful and appropriate to use annual nitrogen fixers.

Nectary plants

Insects are essential for fertilising flowers. This means that specific flowers that are attractive to particular insects can be planted with the intention of attracting them to the garden. This strategy is becoming well known and widely adopted, particularly in recent years to help support honey bees. Ideally flowers should be available for as many months of the year as possible in order to supply the needs of all the insects that would like to set up home in our gardens.

Field beans (April).

Flowers throughout the garden in July, including calendula, phacelia, toad flax, St John's wort, foxglove and roses.

Different plant families have specific characteristics which make them accessible and attractive to particular groups of insects; they include – fennel from the apiaceae family, chicory and dandelion (asteraceae), mints and thymes (lamiaceae).

Aromatic pest confusers

Aromatic pest confusers are highly scented plants, often used as medicinal or culinary herbs. Their volatile scents are able to mask the scent of other plants and send potential predators off course. Many are by definition also both edible and nectary plants.

Insect habitat

Insect habitat is provided by plants that have a diversity of shape and structure and provide a range of options for insects looking to set up home. Some plants are favourite haunts of individual species or a whole gang of different creatures. Ladybirds like nettles and comfrey, beetles adore borage and spiders are happy in the crevices beneath yarrow, fennel and clover. Happily all of these plants also have other functions as dynamic accumulators, nectaries, nitrogen fixers and aromatic pest confusers.

Plant size, shape and form

As well as diverse roles, a polyculture needs diversity of shape and form above and below ground. Like a scaled down forest garden using plants of different heights helps to use the space effectively. One of the main considerations is to find a balance between bigger, brasher and heavier plants, like some of the kales, and more diminutive plants nearby.

As well as sharing the same physical space, plants can also share the garden through the seasons by using the same space at different times. In the woods a flood tide of wild garlic in March and April and blankets of bluebells in April and May eventually subside beneath the new leaves of the tree canopy. Having captured their share of the year's sunlight early on, they lie quietly beneath the trees until the following spring. In the perennial vegetable garden you can likewise plant wild garlic for successional spring harvests and take advantage of the ability of plants like lamb's lettuce and claytonia to grow through the winter months.

There is no hard and fast rule of any kind that perennial vegetables have to be grown in polycultures. However there are advantages to growing in polycultures and it is worth experimenting with them, even if the vegetables themselves are tried out initially in a more conventional setting. Chapter Nine provides a step by step guide to choosing plants for a polyculture and planning their position within it.

Welsh onion about to flower (June). See page 60.

chapter 5

CHOOSING PERENNIAL VEGETABLES

Part One

A vast number of plants are actually edible. However quite a number of these are too bland or too strong or unfamiliar in flavour. Others are troublesome to either grow or to prepare and cook or only produce in small quantities. This brings the realistic choices down to manageable numbers.

The ultimate value of growing perennial vegetables either in the home garden or a forest garden depends on the range, productivity and usefulness of the varieties that are available. Many warm parts of the world rejoice in an abundance of perennials but in the UK (and other similar locations) the cool, temperate, maritime climate constrains the choice of perennial vegetables to three main groups of plants:

- Leafy greens and shoots
- The onion family
- Roots and tubers

Whilst these may not be the most flamboyant and wildly exciting of vegetables, they are important mainstays of vegetable production and include some varieties which possess great nutritional value. Fruiting perennials corresponding to the summer favourites like tomatoes, cucumbers, squashes, beans and peas unfortunately belong to warmer climes. However conventional annual vegetables can always be slotted in with the perennials.

Selecting suitable perennials

I really hope that as a result of reading this book people will begin growing perennial vegetables; I have tried to present them in an accessible way to help you choose suitable varieties for your requirements. The vegetables presented in Chapters Five and Six have been grown in my garden.*

The notes and photographs included here are accurate records of my experience and observation of the best of the perennial vegetables that I have tested using the following criteria:

- They need to have a good flavour although some flavours may be new.

- They must be reliably perennial in my Shropshire garden.

- They must produce reasonable harvests.

- Once established they should be sufficiently robust to be able to grow without any particular attention including being able to cope with slugs.

As this is a personal journey into the world of perennial vegetables I have divided them according to how they have fared in my tender care. Those which have done best are presented in this chapter. Chapter Six contains details of perennials that are known to do well in other locations but have been less successful in my garden. I cannot be sure, but they probably just need different soil and site conditions to do really well. Some of the featured plants have more than one edible part, but they have been categorised according to their perceived primary use. This is not a definitive selection of all possible perennial vegetables, but are representative of those which are currently reasonably easy to find and most useful to grow.[†] After several years of research and trials I am delighted to find that there is a good selection of perennial vegetables to recommend. Seed and plant suppliers are listed in Appendix Two.

Chapter Eight contains recipe suggestions for some of these vegetables, but bear in mind that when trying any new foods it is sensible to take only small quantities at first to ensure that your body is happy with it.

---

[*] Constraints on time and space have meant that I have not yet been able to trial all the possible varieties that might prove suitable. If in the course of continuing experimentation I find other good varieties to grow information on them will be available on my blog: http://annisveggies.wordpress.com

[†] The Plants for a Future database, Jacke and Toensmeier *Volume 2* and *Perennial Vegetables* by Eric Toensmeier and *Creating a Forest Garden* by Martin Crawford have comprehensive lists of every kind of perennial vegetable and plants with many other uses besides

Perennial leafy greens and shoots

These include members of the cabbage and kale family (brassicas), sorrels, and others from miscellaneous plant families. Leaves, shoots and florets from brassicas can be used in place of annual hearted cabbages, kale and sprouting broccoli. Sorrels and their extended family can be used as spinach substitutes, usually cooked, but also sometimes in salads.

In general I have found that the leafy greens prefer the cooler months of the year. Many can tolerate partial shade; indeed my greens planted in shade have fared at least as well as those in the direct sun, and sometimes better. Greens are a fantastic food from autumn to late spring; and although they may stop or slow their growth in the winter they start again in the spring, relishing the bursts of warmth and bright spring sunshine. However in summer, brassicas can become tougher and be subject to some pests and the sorrels can turn bitter with some plants running to seed.

Young kale.

Leafy greens accumulate minerals, including calcium, iron, magnesium, phosphorus, potassium, sodium, zinc, copper, manganese and selenium. I have not been able to find data specifically about perennials, but most leaves will have some, if not all of these. The richer the soil they grow in becomes, the more minerals (and other nutrients) the vegetables will contain and the more benefit will be derived from them.

The brassica family contain a group of twenty or more compounds collectively known as glucosinolates. During cooking and the early stages of digestion these compounds are converted to produce compounds known as isothiocyanates and indoles. Although these names may be somewhat hard to digest the compounds themselves are thought to have a protective effect against cancer.

Kales are also good sources of 'phytonutrients" lutein and zeaxanthin. These are antioxidants and are known to be beneficial to eye health and to have a protective effect against cardiovascular disease, stroke and lung cancer.

Most of the plants below can be obtained as seeds although some (Daubenton's kale) do not flower and have to be propagated by cuttings. Some nurseries supply others as young plants.

* Nutrients contained within a plant

Care of perennial brassicas in general

They are hungry plants requiring fertile soil. They are capable of withstanding harsh conditions and environmental challenges but do need some nurture and protection. I had nine star perennial broccolis that withstood a very wet summer in 2009, a freezing cold winter in 2009-2010 and an onslaught by cabbage white caterpillars. But they went into the still harsher winter of 2010-2011 weakened and having been frozen into snow and ice at temperatures well below zero for over two weeks they unsurprisingly died. Experience has taught me the following:

1. When possible, place brassicas in the most fertile of spots, otherwise build up the fertility around them as much as possible.

2. Not to plant aggressive mineral accumulator plants (for example chicory) in close proximity to hungry brassicas as they will compete in a small patch.

3. During the summer months brassicas in shady conditions grew better than those in full sun. In the shade they may also be less visible to the cabbage white butterfly.

4. But, however well disguised they are, the cabbage white will probably find the plants at some point. However, strong and healthy plants seem to be more resistant but stress such as hot, dry weather seems to make them vulnerable. Chapter Eleven gives details of my strategies for coping with very hungry caterpillars.

5. There is a balance to be had between picking sufficient leaves and shooting stems for food and leaving enough to enable the plant to maintain its health and vigour. Not picking enough can give the plant more stress in summer if it has to support more leaf in dry conditions; it also gives the butterflies a larger surface area to plant their eggs on. Equally picking too much might also stress the plant. However I am inclined towards taking as much as I dare prior to the onset of summer warmth as I would rather eat the leaves myself than leave them for pests or to become bitter.

6. Winter presents a different set of challenges, and unusually harsh conditions will mean that some plants die. My answer from now on is a back up set of young plants, maybe raised from seeds or from cuttings (Daubenton's kale) in the

---

* I have not used netting or any other artificial means to control anything as I wanted to leave things as much as possible to see what happened. Of course this means taking risks with some things and other people may make different choices

autumn and kept in a greenhouse, cold frame, conservatory, shed, garage or even kitchen windowsill if things get really grim outside.

The availability of perennial vegetables

The availability of perennial vegetables varies considerably. Some are widely stocked, others only from specialised suppliers. However, even over the period of my experimentation and writing, a number have become easier to access in the UK and there are plenty of varieties already available to use as a starting point. Appendix Two has details of seed companies and nurseries that I have used. In the meantime I hope that gardeners who do have seeds, cuttings or tubers will share with anyone they know who would like to try them too.

Perennial Green Vegetables – Cabbage Family

Daubenton's Kale
Brassica oleracea var. *ramosa*

During my early attempts to find perennial vegetables Daubenton's kale was an elusive prize. I read conflicting information about it and finding a supplier took some time. I bought my plants from a nursery in France, but they are now more widely available from the UK. I am very pleased to have them as they are lovely. I have two varieties, one has plain green leaves and the other is a pretty variegated plant with pale green leaves edged with cream.

They can become large and are hungry plants which need to be planted in a sunny spot. They have a tendency to become leggy and, if planted in too shady a place, they will just send long stems across the ground. This makes access for slugs and snails much easier. They can become leggy anyway with very many tiny clusters of side shoots and leaves growing along an elongated stem. If this happens I suggest cutting the stems back quite hard and using the side shoots for cuttings to grow more plants. Cuttings tend to take well but grow quite slowly. The plants do not flower so they need to be propagated vegetatively.

Daubenton's kale is in leaf all year round and both varieties start growing very early in the New Year. They do not flower or set seed so energy is available all year for leafy growth. The flavour is milder than some other perennial cabbages and kales. They make pleasant eating all year round, as unlike some other greens they do not seem

Green Daubenton's kale (June).

Variegated Daubenton's kale (July).

Nine star perennial broccoli.

to become bitter in the warmer months. Only the leaves are edible, I have tried the stems, but on the variegated variety even the young stems are too stringy to eat.

They are hardy and tolerant plants but do have their limits. My first plants happily withstood the wet summer of 2009 and harsh winter of early 2010 with no problem. However the even harsher winter of 2010-2011 killed the variegated varieties and all but one small cutting of the plain green variety which had been in a slightly less cold part of the garden. I restocked and the new arrivals grew well despite the dry conditions that prevailed through most of the spring and summer of 2011. I did water them (and the rest of the garden) occasionally when they looked a little wilted. The plan to ensure the winter weather does not defeat them again is to take cuttings in autumn, which if necessary can be taken under cover if the weather is very harsh.

Daubenton's kale happily seems to be less interesting to caterpillars than other brassicas, and in my garden have rarely been targeted. In short Daubenton's kale is attractive, easy to grow, tastes good and well worth obtaining.

Nine Star Perennial Broccoli
Brassica oleracea botrytis asparagoides

This star of a plant is worthy of its name. The centre develops a lovely creamy head, resembling a baby cauliflower whilst side shoots yield beautiful little mini sprouting heads. The heads, leaves, and other flowering shoots can all be eaten and have a flavour of cabbage / kale. It can be steamed as a green vegetable, incorporated into a stir fry, made into soup or spiced up a bit to create some interesting and tasty dishes.

I have read that this plant is only perennial so long as it does not set seed. I wanted to find out if this was the case so during summer 2010 I allowed my plants to flower and set seed to see if they would then die off. Happily they continued to grow!

I wonder if the main problem with allowing them (or any other perennial) to flower and set seed is the corresponding reduction in energy available for plant growth. So it is probably not a good idea, but not the end of the world (or the plant) if it happens. Apart from any other consideration the young flower shoots taste great and it is a waste to leave them.

Nine star perennial broccoli grows into a chunky plant and is probably best well spaced from its neighbours. Like all brassicas it is a hungry plant requiring fertile soil and I mulch mine with garden compost when there is some available.

Generally it is a low maintenance plant, capable of withstanding harsh conditions and environmental challenges but does need some nurture and protection.

Paul and Becky's Asturian Tree Cabbage

I bought seeds of Asturian tree cabbage from a seed company who described it as a heritage variety of perennial kale from Spain. I have been delighted with it. Like other kales it germinates readily and seems easy to please. The leaves are finer in texture and much paler green than the other perennial kales I have and the flavour is correspondingly mild. I have several plants growing in different locations, from sunny to shady and they grew well for several years before succumbing to ultra cold weather in early 2013.

Asturian tree cabbage with lamb's lettuce gone to seed beneath (July).

Walking Stick Kale
Brassica oleracea (Acephala Group)

This is sold more as a novelty plant with the suggestion that the very sturdy stems are used to make walking sticks than as a useful vegetable. However I think they have far wider use than that. The young leaves, flower shoots and stems are nice to eat, although older leaves are tough and have a stronger flavour.

Although they have a reputation for growing very tall, mine have not. They are planted in quite shady corners and have flopped over and bent towards

Walking stick kale growing in shrub border (July).

the light. Some have stems running along the ground with leaves shooting skyward. They have done well and provided reliable greens through much of the year.

Through March, April and May my plants sprouted flower heads which I picked off and ate. They continued trying to flower faster than I could eat the shoots and eventually I decided to allow them to flower and set seed. By mid August the plants were bearing both flowering shoots and new leaf shoots as well!

Walking stick kale germinates easily from seed; mine took ten days outside in March and was not any quicker when started in February the following year when it took four weeks. During the wet summer of 2009 it was subject to attack from armies of caterpillars. I stood back, watched and took no action just waiting to see what the outcome would be and there did not seem to be any long term damage. It then continued to stand bravely through the harsh winter of 2009-2010 and came into new growth around February even in a harsh, cold winter. It served well throughout 2010 but was eventually felled by the excessive cold of 2010-11.

This is a vegetable which is generally easy to grow and maintain. It is readily available as seed and well worth trying, particularly when starting out with perennial vegetables.

Wild Cabbage
Brassica oleracea

This is another star plant; being wild it is tough and persistent! I raised my first batch of plants from seeds sown outside, first in February, just to see how tough it might be. They took four weeks to germinate, but I was impressed that they did. A second batch was sown in mid March and germinated in under a fortnight.

Wild cabbage growing under apple tree, photograph taken at head height (September).

The plants grew well, were repotted in May and planted out in June. By mid August when the other brassicas were looking decidedly pale and lacklustre it was untroubled by pests and growing well. It was planted in a fairly shady spot as the best places were already taken so it began growing quite slowly but ended up becoming extremely vigorous and large.

The references say it is biennial or perennial. Unfortunately my first batch died in the winter of 2010-2011. The second batch produced two plants which grew enormous in their first summer (2012) and survived the incredibly harsh conditions of March 2013 that did kill other plants. I have taken cuttings and also allowed them to flower and set seed as they are clearly very vigorous and hardy and I want lots more of them!

The flavour is quite strong, but for those who enjoy cabbagey flavours it is very nice. The one down side is that the seeds are not widely available at present. I obtained mine from a European supplier, details of which are in Appendix Two.

Other Perennial Kales

There are other perennial kales which I have not yet tried; Trouve Tronchuda a loose leafed variety from Portugal, Taunton Dean, presumably British, and ehrwiger kohl, presumably German. All my experiments lead me to the belief that most kales will quite happily perennialise and Chapter Six has more details of this.

Wild Rocket
Eruca sativa

What a plant! Wild rocket is easy to grow and very hardy. It germinates readily from seed and makes rapid growth. It is in leaf all year and from my observation it grows for much of that time. It is not fussy regarding soil type. References say that it is an annual plant but it lasts for years, flowering and setting seed each year with no ill effects.

My original plants came equally well through several wet summers and one very dry one, plus two horribly cold winters. In the early spring of 2011 after a punishing winter that killed neighbouring kales the plants were small and looked weak, but once milder weather came they quickly picked up again. They eventually succumbed having been frozen in snow for weeks in early 2013. Their replacements are doing well!

Wild rocket.

A mature plant will froth and tilt and bubble about, producing masses of leaves. If anything, it is a bit too eager to grow and sprawls about sometimes swamping its neighbours. This tendency probably makes it ideal for a forest garden where it may have more room for such untidy behaviour. The answer is to cut it back firmly when it gets exuberant during the spring and summer and use the cuttings in the kitchen. If there is more growth than we can eat (highly likely) I just drop the surplus back down nearby as a green mulch.

When eaten raw wild rocket is very peppery and hot. It can be used as a salad leaf, but is best used in small amounts well mixed with milder leaves. However it can also be eaten cooked – steamed for a short time. But again I tend to use small quantities mixed with milder greens. Alternatively its flavour is radically toned down when made into soup together with milder ingredients such as in the recipe in Chapter Eight.

I have not been able to find any references that detail its nutritional value, but the chances are that it is high in minerals; and being a member of the brassica family, it is likely to contain beneficial phytonutrients.

Most of my wild rocket plants are growing in sunny spots though some are happy in semi shade. This year they have been growing in polycultures alongside oca, Jerusalem artichoke, garlic and chives but are so easy going that they are probably likely to do well in any company.

Wild rocket is also extremely resistant to slugs and other pests even when neighbouring plants have been affected. I don't think I have seen any pest damage at all apart from a few leaves with cabbage white butterfly eggs on in a new polyculture patch in its first year.

The strong flavour means nobody probably wants masses of wild rocket plants for food, although they would usefully fill spare space for as long as necessary. Overall they are very useful and highly recommended.

Perennial Green Vegetables – Other Plant Families

Asparagus
Asparagus officinalis

Asparagus is one of the few perennial vegetables that needs no introduction. It is widely relished as a spring time luxury; having your own supply saves money and allows you to relish the superb flavour of freshly picked asparagus which is far better than asparagus bought from the market or supermarket. It is also a very attractive plant producing a mass of beautiful, delicate, ferny foliage up to 2m tall.

To enable the plants to establish and build up strength new plants should not be harvested in the first year, and sadly only sparingly in the second year. Thereafter they can be harvested for six to eight weeks from mid spring.

On heavy soils or those with a tendency to water logging asparagus should be planted onto raised beds or ridges to provide better drainage. Mine is growing in the first polyculture patch which has been raised quite high over the years with the addition of large amounts of mulch. It is in the sun and I have not tried it in shade.

I cheated and bought my asparagus in a pot! The normal method is either by seed or from crowns. In the autumn cut them down to 2.5cm above ground level and mulch again. Plants may require staking in windy situations. Any general vegetable reference book will give cultivation details and information about different varieties available and their relative merits.

Buckler Leaved Sorrel
Rumex scutatus

Buckler leaved sorrel is an exuberant plant. It sprawls about, filling in the ground between its neighbours with a profusion of delicate and attractive leaves. I bought mine as a plant which I have split and moved without any difficulty. It has been in the garden for five years and thrived despite every type of trying weather over that time. Apart from its tendency to grow rapidly and sprawl on nearby plants, it is no trouble at all. I keep it under control by pulling or cutting away the excess when it starts to bump into neighbouring plants and using as a green mulch nearby. It has a deep taproot and I am therefore assuming it may well play a role as mineral accumulator if you use the surplus growth as mulch or in the compost.

It has a lovely sharp lemony tang and its acidity means that it works well in a green salad or a soup. Sorrel is one of the traditional greens used in spring for cleansing the body in herbal medicine and is perhaps particularly valuable at that time of year. However like all sorrels it contains oxalic acid and should only be eaten in small amounts.

Buckler leaf sorrel would work well as a ground cover plant in a forest garden where its undemanding nature and sprawling, rampaging habit would be a very positive

Buckler leaved sorrel on edge of polyculture (July).

Sea beet (October).

Nettles growing with mint (October).

attribute. In a smaller patch these attributes need watching, but it is nevertheless a useful plant.

Sea Beet
Beta vulgaris maritima

Somewhat unusually for a wild plant this one has a nice mild taste. Seeds were sown in early spring, potted up in May and planted out into the polyculture towards the end of June. They did not all survive this transfer but by the end of summer one plant in particular had grown into a very handsome clump measuring 60 x 60cm. It was growing in light shade. Although the flavour is generally mild if they bolt in the sunshine their flavour will become bitter.

Stinging Nettle
Urtica dioica

I can just about remember a time when I saw stinging nettles as an enemy. Now I regard them as a great plant to have in the garden. Whilst the nettle has become almost an emblem for foraging and many people are aware that it can be eaten, it is still probably somewhat eccentric to allow (or possibly) encourage it to grow in one's garden.

Nevertheless I have nettles growing near a number of the perennial brassicas. I aim to keep them roughly level or slightly below the brassicas during the time when cabbage white butterflies are in the garden as they may be able to provide some cover from this undoubted pest. When I cut them back I generally just drop the cuttings on the ground beside where they have been growing to replenish the soil with the nutrients they have accumulated. I also leave them to grow on the edges of the garden and during spring and early summer cut them back and deposit the cuttings wherever I need some mulch or nutrients. Their fine, soft leaves readily decompose.

They can of course get out of hand, but keeping them cut is effectively harvesting them to feed the garden and is quicker than removing them. If a clump has become unruly and needs to be removed I have found that the soil in most polyculture patches has become so soft and fluffy that they are quite easy to pull up.

In spring we eat nettle soup, which is delicious, and lightly steamed they make a fabulous spinach substitute with a truly lovely flavour. They can also be cooled and chopped and then added to egg dishes, sauces or risotto. They appear early in the year and as soon as the new year has come I start peering to see if the young leaves have begun to grow.

Wood Sorrel
Oxalis acetosella

This is a delightful wild woodland plant with edible leaves that can be picked all year round although they are most useful during the winter months. Like all sorrels it has a sharp, lemony tang and should be used in small amounts. It is very attractive and perfect for a woodland setting or as a ground cover in a shady spot.

Wood sorrel growing beneath apple tree (April).

Perennial Onions

The onion (*Allium*) family is huge! Incredibly they are all edible, even those normally grown as ornamental plants. I have included quite a lot as I love them, both to look at and to eat. Small young leaves can be used in salad as spring onion substitutes and larger tougher leaves cooked as leek substitutes.

All parts are edible; in addition they are all aromatic pest confusers and have ornamental flowers which attract insects. With different species flowering through the course of the year there are plenty of reasons to incorporate lots of them.

Nutritionally alliums contain allyl sulphides which confer health benefits. This group of compounds have an antibacterial effect; they also inhibit the production of carcinogenic (cancer causing) compounds. Studies show that areas where the population consumes high levels of garlic and onions have lower rates of stomach cancer.[*] Additionally allyl sulphides are known to reduce cholesterol.

This family of plants uses a variety of means to multiply, some produce seed, others produce miniature 'bulbils' on stems and others divide at the base of the clump. These properties can be usefully exploited in a perennial vegetable patch each time a plant multiplies it gives an edible portion for no work!

Chives
Allium schoenoprasum

Chives are of course very well known and widely grown herbs and most gardens probably feature a small clump of chives somewhere. But do not let familiarity lead to overlooking them as they are very useful in the perennial vegetable patch. They accumulate calcium, magnesium and potassium in their leaves which are all valuable nutrients.

Chives are early starters giving onion greens for salad from late winter / early spring to well on in the autumn. The pink flowers are also edible and attract lots of bees. As spring moves on and other plants begin to appear it's so easy to stop paying attention to the chives; but if you want to maximise the output from your garden make sure you continue to pick them all summer long and into autumn until they finally settle down for a well earned rest. A good handful of chives weigh 50g which is enough for two days of salad in our household. With sufficient plants picking 50g three times a week, every week for six months would yield 3.6kg!

[*] *Human Nutrition and Dietetics* 10th edition; J. S. Garrow, W. Philip T. James and A. Ralph; Churchill Livingstone, 2000.

Chives in flower front left, wild strawberry centre front, scorzonera and land cress going to seed behind (July).

Few flowered leek, with lamb's lettuce underneath and scorzonera back left (March).

They grow up to about 0.3m high in all soil types, but do need a sunny position in moist but well drained soil. They can be grown from seed sown into individual pots in spring and planted out when large enough or can be propagated by dividing existing clumps. It is a good idea to divide clumps every few years anyway to maintain their vigour. Dot them about wherever you can fit them in.

Chives are easily acquired, practically indestructible, bulk up quite quickly and really cannot be praised too highly!

I have also tried growing Giant Chives (*Allium schoenoprasum sibiricum*) which are one of a number of chives that are available. They grow to about 0.3m in height and produce leaves for much of the year. I obtained plants and put them quite close to a clump of ordinary chives. During the first summer the giants were initially smaller but towards the end of the growing season began to put on more growth. The leaves have a stronger flavour than ordinary chives.

Everlasting Onion
Allium cepa 'Perutile'

This is a low growing perpetual spring onion. It forms clumps but never flowers. I will be getting more of these useful plants!

Few Flowered Leek
Allium paradoxum

This is another lovely onion which appears in spring. It is a delightfully pretty woodland plant with edible leaves, flowers and bulbs. According to some sources this plant is considered to be invasive, but if you want to eat it, the habit of fast multiplying is surely an advantage.

Garlic Chives
Allium tuberosum

Garlic chives are another attractive member of the onion family. They grow to 0.3m tall and are in leaf from early spring to late autumn. The flattish white flower heads are produced late summer and autumn and are also edible. Garlic chives like a sunny home, with a well-drained moist soil of any type.

They can be propagated by sowing seed in pots in spring and planting out when they have developed sufficiently or by dividing existing clumps.

The leaves and flowers are edible, usually raw, but they can be lightly cooked. As the name suggests their flavour is oniony with overtones of garlic.

Nodding Wild Onion
Allium cernuum

This is another lovely plant – with delicate and attractive dusky pink flowers and leaves that are somewhat triangular in section. They are well worth including in any garden just for their loveliness. Nodding onion does not require any particular soil type but does need a sunny position in moist, well-drained soil. It grows up to 0.5m tall, but mine are considerably smaller and look delicate and somewhat diminutive growing beside some burly Welsh onions.

The bulb, leaves and flowers are all edible raw or cooked. The leaves are available from spring to autumn, flowers in the summer and when I dug a couple up to find the bulb, I found only a long (10cm) piece of underground stem, like a subterranean spring onion. I find the leaves have no flavour but I do like the white underground stem. It compares well with a conventional spring onion, although a little chewy.

I have grown nodding onion through many growing seasons without any problems. They flower in summer and will happily self-seed, or you can harvest the seed to plant in planned locations. They also appear to divide at the base to form more plants.

My plants have been through two very wet summers, two very cold winters and latterly a very dry summer with no apparent ill effects. I have left them to their own

Graceful nodding wild onion in flower on left flanked by Welsh onion on right (June).
Perpetual leek (April).
Three cornered leek (April).

devices and not provided any care, again with no ill effects. As a wild plant, nodding onion seems well able to take the proverbial rough with the smooth and just keep going. For this reason it is probably well suited to any relatively unmanaged area such as a forest garden.

Perpetual Leek / Poireau perpétuel
Allium porrum

This is an intriguing plant I spied on the website for the French supplier of Daubenton's kales several years ago. It has taken some time to become established in my garden but it is now growing strongly making an ever larger clump. It appears early in the spring and dies down at the end of spring. The individual stems are like very baby leeks and don't seem to get larger as the clump ages. Another useful plant which never flowers and is truly perennial.

Three Cornered Leek
Allium triquetrum

The three cornered leek is presumably named after its distinctive stem which is triangular in cross section. It is one of the very first indicators in my garden that winter is fading as it puts its early leaves above ground at about the same time as the crocuses, if not the snowdrops as I have seen them above ground in December! They grow rapidly, forming small plants somewhat like very miniature leeks – the stem has a short length of white (below ground) topped by green (above ground) and pretty outer leaves curling round in a circle. It produces exquisite white flowers similar in shape to bluebells; if it were only for decoration I would love it, but being edible as well what more could you want?

The height of plants varies according to position and fertility. They certainly grow much taller – up to 40cm – in rich soil, even in the shade. However they also seed and grow into very awkward spaces in my garden between rocks where you would never be able to plant deliberately and grow there in very little depth of soil.

The leaf / stem flavour is a mild onion flavour and it can be used raw or cooked.

It is a rampant self-seeder which has earned it a reputation as a troublesome weed; but as a food plant that reproduces vigorously. Personally I can't have enough of them!

Tree Onion
Allium cepa proliferum

Tree onions are easy to grow and reliably perennial. They can become tall plants of a metre or so in height, although mine are about half a metre. Their distinguishing characteristic is that they form small bulbs (bulbils) at the top of the main stem towards the end of summer. If left alone the stems they are borne on gradually bend and fall to the ground and the bulbils take root, thus propagating more plants; or you can remove them and plant them where required.

Leafy onion greens are available throughout the growing season but removing too many leaves could reduce the production of bulbils. A bulb also forms at the base of the plant which can also be eaten cooked or raw. I find the flavour quite mild though other sources say they are strongly flavoured.

They prefer a good, fertile soil in a sunny position that should not be allowed to dry out. I have tried growing them in the shade when sunny space was at a premium. They grew slowly, but were generally okay, doing better after I moved them into the sun.

At present tree onions are not too hard to source. However they tend to come singly and it either takes time to propagate more or money to buy more in the first place. Some suppliers provide bulbils and others established plants.

Welsh Onion
Allium fistulosum

Welsh onions are reliable and hardy, and produce plenty of growth from early spring through to autumn. The leaves have a mild onion flavour and can be eaten raw or cooked. The thickened stems of larger plants can also be eaten, but these are hot and best cooked.

Bulbils forming on tree onion and growing entwined with a tomato plant, yarrow on left (June).

Wild garlic (April).

They are tolerant of different soil types, but need a sunny situation and soil that does not dry out. They grow to half a metre tall (or possibly more) and make attractive plants as they hold high their lovely flower heads in summer. They seem to respond well to being given a rich soil to grow in – there are marked differences between plants in different parts of my garden. Those in the most fertile parts have grown particularly large. They can then form a solid, thickened stem and a swollen bulb base and also start to split into new plants. Sometimes the hollow stems can get rather floppy, falling and straggling over and under their neighbours but I have found that the stronger and healthier the plant the more upright they will be. To harvest leaves I cut them off as required. To harvest the swollen base of the plant I cut it off at ground level.

To grow from seed, sow in spring and plant out when they have made good-sized plants. They can be attacked by slugs, but good strong plants are able to withstand this. They also self-seed round the garden quite readily. The name Welsh onion is a bit of a misnomer as they actually originate from Siberia; hence they are particularly tough and well able to withstand cold winters.

There is a variety of red Welsh onions which initially did well but sadly do not appear to like my garden, I think it is probably just too shady and damp.

Wild Garlic
Allium ursinum

Wild garlic is for me the confirmation that spring is well on the way. It begins to emerge in March and by early April is producing abundant fountains of shiny, vivid green leaves. Its bursts into early abundance while other foods are quite scarce and serves as a welcome reminder of the vitality and fertility of the forces gathering momentum below ground.

Picking the leaves and flowers of wild garlic is one of my favourite treats in early spring. The leaves can be eaten raw or cooked and have a mild onion flavour. I eat the buds and flowers raw and savour their heat. They also look great in salads and as a garnish on other foods. If you have plenty to spare the roots are also edible.

It is very easy to grow given a damp and partly shaded site and will seed itself around. If it is left unpicked, or only lightly picked in the first couple of years, it will soon grow into substantial clumps.

Perennial Roots and Tubers

How I love potatoes! In Britain we have such a commitment to and dependence upon the potato and yet there are other lovely roots and tubers out there that we can equally fall in love with. Root vegetables are plants that have adapted themselves to store energy in their roots as sugars and starches for future use. They may be taproots like carrots and parsnips, tubers like potatoes, or sometimes corms like the tiger nut, *Cyperus esculentus*.

A surprising variety of plants actually have edible roots. Some were eaten in Britain in the past, but with the industrialisation of agriculture they were effectively lost; others have arrived more recently and may be entirely unfamiliar. I have to say that I have enjoyed experimenting with new roots more than anything else, in part because of the novelty of new plants and foods.

The contribution that root vegetables make to diet is primarily as a source of sugars and starches which provide energy (calories) for fuelling the body. Calorific foods get a bad press when they are associated with weight gain but in the correct amounts they are vital to a healthy diet. Some perennial root vegetables are rich in inulin rather than starch. This is a sugar like compound, but one which does not raise blood sugar and is therefore suitable for diabetics. It is also a 'prebiotic' as it feeds and promotes the growth of the beneficial intestinal bacteria known as 'probiotics'.

Most perennial roots are harvested in the autumn or early winter when the plant has become dormant. Tap rooted species which grow in clumps can be divided and replanted and tubers and corms can be replanted at the time of harvest. Exceptions that are somewhat tender and need to be replanted in spring are clearly identified.

Chinese Artichoke
Stachys affinis

This is a root vegetable from the mint family of plants. It grows to approximately 0.5m high and spreads underground by means of runners to form a clump which will continue to grow if left unchecked. The tubers are small, from 5cm long by 2cm wide. They can be eaten raw or cooked, with no need to peel, and have a mild pleasant flavour.

Chinese artichoke will grow in most soils planted in a sunny or partly shaded location. I have tried both light and deep shade and whilst they will grow in shade, in the deepest shade they have only attained 20cm whereas those in a sunnier

Clump of Chinese artichokes growing with yam and shallots (August).

Earth nut pea climbing a hedge (June).

spot are sturdier and 50cm tall. They can be planted in March and left in place until harvesting what is required from October onwards as needed.

I have tried to over winter them by saving them inside in a cool dry place for replanting in spring and also by leaving them in the garden. The saved tubers withered to nothing and just about disappeared but those in the garden survived an atrociously cold winter in ground that was frozen solid for weeks.

All round they are highly recommended. In experiments, a polyculture of Chinese artichoke, shallots and earth nut pea were quite happy growing together. They have also intermingled quite happily near the kales (but not too close to avoid root disturbance when the tubers are dug) and some are snuggling up to a gooseberry bush and clumps of oca.

Earth Nut Pea
Lathyrus tuberosus

This is a pretty, nitrogen-fixing climber growing to approximately 75cm. It is characteristic of the pea family to which it belongs with delicate leaves and delightful mid pink flowers from July to September. I grew my plants from seed obtained from a supplier in Germany. Seed purchased and first sown one year were still viable the next. Pre-soaked seeds were sown in small pots towards the end of March and appeared just over three weeks later in mid April.

They have proved to be hardy and reliable plants which I have grown in the garden and in pots. They seem happy wherever they are and have grown beneath gigantic Jerusalem artichokes; in a pot with oca or onions, in a shady polyculture with Chinese artichoke and shallots, up a hedge and in a flower border with marigolds! They will clearly grow in the shade, but do grow larger in the sun.

Sources say they are susceptible to slugs and some re-emerging plants have been a bit nibbled and I have kept young plants in pots until they were at least 15cm tall. In dry summers, in common with other peas they have had some mildew but this has not prevented the seeds from ripening or damaged the tubers.

They produce a string of small round tubers meaning some can be eaten and the remainder replanted. I boiled them and tasted them plain– they have a firm texture and mild, pleasant flavour which I am sure is capable of complementing many dishes or meals.

Earth nut pea is easy to grow and easy to save the seed to grow more. In addition they attract lots of insects and fix nitrogen. Even if you could not eat the tubers they would be lovely plants to have and their edibility makes them just perfect. They are well worth growing if you get the chance. I am working on saving as much seed as I can and increasing my stock so that eventually I will be able to have a good supply of tubers. Currently the seeds are available from Europe.[*]

Groundnut
Apios americana

This plant tends to be known first by its Latin name, *Apios americana*, and secondarily by a range of others including ground nut. It is a nitrogen-fixing climber that is likely to grow to over a metre in height and produces strings of golf ball sized underground tubers. It is a hardy plant capable of surviving cold winters, but not guaranteed to come through the harshest conditions.

I coveted it for a long time before finally tracking down my first very tiny plant from a flower nursery. It is also now available from suppliers of perennial vegetables. The first plant was minute on arrival in spring and did not fare well for a long time despite my best nurturing. In the end a cloche placed over the pot gave it the extra cosseting it needed and it took off. Once it was 30cm or so high with a number of climbing stems, it was planted out near the Jerusalem artichokes. Some of the leaves were nibbled, but generally it grew well. I decided it was too risky to dig that one up after a single season in the ground and left it in situ hoping it would reappear in spring. After a very cold winter it eventually reappeared in late spring by which time I had bought another. This plant was much larger and healthier.

[*] www.magicgardenseeds.com

Ground nut (October).   Jerusalem artichoke (August).

That summer was uncharacteristically dry and they both grew to about one metre high but with little foliage. Plant number one, growing in shade, produced a single tuber, although there may have been others I did not find. Plant number two produced a couple of tubers joined together, plus a couple of string-like roots at the tip of which new tubers were forming. Even though it was December it seemed that it had not finished its growing cycle so I replanted this one and harvested the single.

Groundnut has a very firm, if not hard, texture before cooking, perhaps a little firmer than swede. After boiling it had a firm, somewhat dry and floury texture (which I liked) with a rather bland taste. It was better covered in spicy homemade tomato sauce and is I suspect the kind of vegetable that absorbs flavours well. It is undemanding in the garden, clearly hardy, nitrogen fixing and I will definitely grow more of this.

Jerusalem Artichoke
Helianthus tuberosus

Jerusalem artichokes are one of the few perennial vegetables that are already quite well known. They are hardy and produce good yields, growing in most soils. They are said to prefer a sunny situation although I have several clumps in different positions some in shade and some in sun. The difference in top growth even within a few feet is marked. One clump is growing in semi shade, but rich, well mulched soil. These plants tower skyward and measure between 2.25m and 2.5m in height, although this is reduced somewhat as they are leaning away from the fence towards the light. Standing amongst them is like being in a mini forest! Another clump, which is planted in sun but on the edge of the patch where I have not mulched much and which has been pretty dry this summer, are from 0.8m to 1m tall with much paler leaves and slender stems. For preference I would plant them in a sunny spot but will happily put them in shade as well if that is all that is available.

Plant them either as whole or partial tubers approximately 50g in weight to a depth of 10cm. Do this as early as possible in spring, as late planting reduces crop size. Slugs are partial to young growth, and may scissor it off repeatedly at ground level, so be vigilant.

Harvest from autumn through the winter; frosts sweeten the tubers which can apparently then be eaten raw, although I have not tried this. After the first year, leaving some tubers in the ground after taking what is required for the kitchen will ensure that you continue to enjoy these amazingly easy vegetables. Mine tend to come up in May.

The tubers contain high levels of inulin, which is a 'fructo-oligosaccharide' and has the same building blocks as sugar, but in a form that some people have difficulty digesting; hence they have a reputation for causing flatulence. The good news is that inulin is known to be a beneficial 'prebiotic' and as such are food for the beneficial bacteria that live in the gut. A supply of prebiotics, whether by diet or supplement is known to benefit general health.[*]

Different varieties are available from stockists, the tubers of the 'common' Jerusalem artichoke are knobbly and irregular, Fuseau is a variety that produces larger, smoother skinned tubers.

Mashua
Tropaeolum tuberosum

Mashua is an incredibly vigorous climber. It is a member of the same family as the familiar garden nasturtiums as is readily confirmed by the shape of its leaves. In good soil it readily climbs and scrambles over the neighbouring plants. Its foliage and flowers are very attractive and it would not look out of place in a flower border. Its vigorous habit would also make it an excellent plant to grow up anything you wanted temporarily disguised during the summer months.

I plant the tubers in pots in March and transfer the young plants to the garden after the frosts have finished. Like oca, the foliage dies back when the autumn frosts arrive. I leave the plants to die down and harvest a couple of weeks later. It is possible to have very high yields but this seems to be somewhat dependent on prevailing weather conditions. It may well be possible to leave tubers in the garden over the winter. I did this accidentally and they survived and came into growth in the late spring.

[*] http://onlinelibrary.wiley.com/doi/10.1111/j.1365-2036.2006.03042.x/full

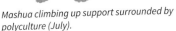

Mashua climbing up support surrounded by polyculture (July).

Oca in the foreground, yacon behind (August).

Unfortunately mashua is attractive to cabbage white butterflies but this can be managed by paying close attention if any butterflies are spotted and checking the leaves for eggs. It is a simple matter then to remove them by cutting the leaf off. There are so many leaves on this very, very vigorous plant that it makes no difference.

Mashua is best cooked, although it is edible raw. I roast them with other root vegetables. I have not tried them raw, apparently the taste is peppery and unpalatable to some people.

Oca
Oxalis tuberosa

Oca makes a very attractive plant and bears a crop of lemony tubers at the end of the growing season. The plants take a little while to get growing in the spring, but by summer become strong and trouble free. After they have reached about half a metre in height they seem to find it hard to support their own weight and can start to sprawl sideways; therefore they do take up quite a lot of room.

I have been digging up and storing tubers for eating and some to replant the following year but last winter I missed a few. These appeared in the garden towards the end of May none the worse for having spent the winter outside. In future years I will probably leave some in place and save others inside.

The stored tubers have been kept cool and dry during the winter, loosely wrapped in a cotton cloth in a frost-free garage. In early spring I plant them into pots (or sooner if they are starting to sprout) and keep the pots in a light frost-free area. Once the danger of frost has passed I plant them outside in the polyculture patches. Some plants have been in reasonably sunny places, others were deliberately placed in shade. Shady conditions do not seem to have been disadvantageous as plants in all situations have produced tubers for harvest.

Oca is sensitive to the length of day. I have read in different sources that it:

- Starts to form tubers once the days are 12 hours long and takes six to eight months to complete this process

and also

- That tubers only begin to form after the autumn equinox in September

These may be two sides of the same coin, I am not sure. However I do know that I leave my plants until the frost has killed the top growth (this may take several frosts) and then some weeks afterwards before harvesting. Once the foliage has died it can be quite hard to locate where the base of the plant actually was and, as this is where you need to look for the tubers it is a good idea to put a stick or other marker in the ground before they disappear completely.

Yields per plant have been quite variable, but not for any very clear reason. Some plants have yielded just over 100g and others almost 1kg, with most falling between these figures.

Scorzonera
Scorzonera hispanica

Scorzonera is easily obtained and quite widely known as a root crop. However, although it is capable of living for years, once dug up (and eaten), as we normally do, it is clearly finished. Some sources recommend growing it for perennial salad leaves. I do not particularly like the leaves raw, but cooked they are rather nice with a mild flavour. They need a little more cooking than cabbage or kale leaves but are a perfectly good addition to a dish of mixed green vegetables and would probably do well in soup.

More interestingly I have been growing scorzonera as a perennial root crop. I sowed seed in spring and planted the seedlings out at about 10cm height. They grew without any trouble, with no evidence of any pests or disease. I dug the plants up in the autumn and used most of the root, but kept back and replanted a short section from the top. I retained the leaves but cut them right back to approximately 4cm in order to reduce stress on the much shortened root. They survived through winter with no ill effects and began to grow strongly again in March. By mid April they sent up flower shoots. I left them to flower, collected the seed and waited for harvest time to see if they would be edible or perhaps have gone woody in texture.

By early October the foliage was dying back so I dug up the roots. They had grown well and were not woody at all when cooked. Each year I have replanted a portion of the roots and note that they sometimes produce another plant or plants beside the original as well. Each plant grows a good-sized root, up to 25cm long. I really like this vegetable and each year have added to the stock with new plants from seed. It grows best in sun but is also fine in semi shade.

Skirret
Sium sisarum

Skirret is a member of the carrot family and is an old vegetable that has largely fallen out of use. It features clumps of taproots rather than just one. It is this quality which makes it an easily managed perennial vegetable. I use the largest roots for the kitchen and gently tease apart the rest of the clump. It readily splits up and these new clumps are then replanted for next year. In addition the flowers produced through the summer attract insects and have an ethereal beauty as they float in the air above the polyculture.

I grew mine from seed and they have been one of the most undemanding plants in the garden. As I knew they were reliably perennial I relegated them first to a very inauspicious place in shade. They produced reasonable roots and to see if they would produce more I replanted them in a slightly less dingy spot. So this year I moved them a little, but not enough to increase the yields significantly. If I ever get more space in the sun I will surely grow more skirret there. In the meantime it is doing fine in part shade.

Scorzonera regrowing for second year (April).

The same scorzonera plant harvested in October.

Skirret in flower (July).

Yacon entwined with Trail of Tears French bean (October).

Young yam plant mingling with asparagus (August).

The roots my plants have produced to date are decidedly thin, about the thickness of my little finger! Peeling them would have been impossible, so I scrubbed (most) of the soil off and popped them in a tray of roasted vegetables. Lovely! A very mild parsnip flavour, but without the after taste that some people dislike in parsnip. This is a delightfully easy to grow, hardy and tolerant plant. It will withstand being stuck in frozen snow for weeks, grow in shade but probably much prefers sun if it can get it. I will certainly be increasing my stock of them.

Yacon
Polymnia edulis

Yacon is a tuberous root vegetable that originates from South America with large edible tubers hanging from the plant which are similar in appearance to white potatoes. Growing closer to the stem are smaller, distinctly different tubers which are used for propagation.

I dig the plant up, harvest the edible tubers first and then remove the others. This is not always very easy as they can be virtually welded to the stem and all in a tight knit clump. I have resorted to cutting this up with a knife. Some plants also have shoots starting below ground and I carefully remove these with some root as well. Each of the tubers (or cut sections or shoots) are planted in barely damp / almost dry compost in individual pots (I use large yogurt pots) and kept in a frost free place over the winter. Mine go in the conservatory where they can get light as they can begin to grow soon after planting. However this is very variable and some take months to appear whilst others do not grow.

Growth is always frustratingly slow, but they have to stay in until danger of frost has passed. Once in the garden they continue to grow slowly, but by August they do seem to go faster. They are tender to frost so I harvest them just after the first frosts have felled the top growth.

Yields are impressive and the tubers keep very well. I store them in a theoretically cool, dry frost free garage, but it can be very cold and in very wet weather, not all that dry. Nevertheless the yacon generally continue to keep well.

Yacon is edible both raw and cooked. It has a crispy texture and some people say a fruity taste resembling pears. The tubers become sweeter and less starchy if they are kept for a while before eating. All in all this is a fantastic plant which richly deserves to be much more widely grown and eaten. Because of the additional tubers made each year it is easy to increase your stock and to pass them on to other people as well.

Yam, Chinese
Dioscorea batatas

Yam, Japanese
Dioscorea japonica

In many other countries yams are a staple food but in the UK they are likely to be considered too exotic to grow. In fact the two species above – Chinese yam and Japanese yam – are very hardy. They are potentially very valuable perennial vegetables as they can give high yields and have good flavour.

Yams are generally supplied to be grown from 'tubercles' which are mini aerial tubers produced from between the leaf axils of a mature plant. They are sown in early spring and planted out in late spring. Although my yams (both Chinese and Japanese) have grown, they have produced disappointingly small tubers which were at best akin to a small to medium potato and not at all like the massive ones I have read about. However they are very hardy having survived three exceptionally cold winters and I plan to continue growing them to see if eventually I can increase the yield as they are pleasant to eat with a mild flavour and dense but floury texture. Even if they do not produce any food they have such attractive foliage they are worth keeping for that alone.

Red veined
sorrel (May).
See page 89.

chapter 6

CHOOSING PERENNIAL VEGETABLES

Part Two

The previous chapter detailed perennial vegetables I have found most useful and rewarding so far; but as previously mentioned there are many more to choose from. This chapter details some which have not made it into my list of favourites for a number of reasons:

- Some I was unable to grow successfully – but I know other people do.

- Some I have not yet had time to try.

- Some I have grown, but which turned out to have a none too pleasant flavour to my taste buds. However we are all different and other people might enjoy them.

However, to begin with I wanted to mention my experiments with vegetables, which are, as far as I am aware, universally known and grown as annuals, but actually can be grown perennially. My experiments with this are on-going as I have more species I wish to try. Nevertheless the results to date have clearly demonstrated the value of using 'annuals' as perennials.

Annuals That Can Be Grown As Perennials

Sometimes the accepted classifications of plants as annual, biennial and perennial relate more to how they are used in conventional gardening rather than their actual biological properties. Years ago I grew some lovely wallflowers (classified as biennial), which are usually removed by gardeners after flowering in their second year of growth. I don't know if I just couldn't bring myself to take out plants that had not died or if I was saving on work but they were cut back after flowering and left in place. They continued to repeat flower for years afterwards. With this in mind as my perennial vegetable experiment continued I have tried using some vegetables normally grown as annuals to see what happens if they are left in place.

Garlic
Allium sativum

I have been growing garlic perennially for a number of years, initially because we use so much in cooking that it seemed better to grow it than buy it. My approach has been somewhat random and this tolerant plant has accepted being planted anywhere I feel like. It is vital to harvest the plants as they start to die down in the summer as the bulbs are mature at this stage and if left longer they cannot be found amongst the other plants in the polyculture. I lift them then and sort them choosing the larger ones for the kitchen and replant the others.

Raised this way they do not grow into huge bulbs pregnant with fat cloves as they should if grown conventionally, but they do have a much stronger flavour than shop bought cloves. Some bulbs do not split into cloves and we tend to use these for cooking rather than replant, but it is not always easy to tell and I don't think it matters much.

Alternatively garlic can be left in the ground from year to year. It will then form a clump of stems resembling young leeks. I cut them at the base, leaving some shoots intact and others to regrow from ground level. When steamed they have a lovely mild garlicky / leeky flavour.

Many varieties are available to buy and gardening books say that you should obtain disease resistant bulbs for planting. I cheated and used organic cloves from the supermarket because they were a lot cheaper. Grown in polycultures there have been no problems with disease.

Leek
Allium porrum

I left some annual leeks in the ground to see what would happen. They predictably ran to very pretty flower heads in the second summer and the following spring sent up slim baby leek stems. This year they have yielded tender young oniony greens from February to June and reappeared in late November. They are quite small and you have to keep a watchful eye out as they can be hidden from view if they are growing in a polyculture. I have a couple of plants I use as mental markers and look for the leeks by them.

The first year I regrew leeks I mistakenly thought that if they were left they would fatten up, but instead they began to produce flower stalks which were too tough to eat.

Young garlic in flower bed (November).   Leek regrowing for the third year (May).   Shallots and self sown forget me nots (foreground) oca behind (July).

I now make sure to harvest them young. I have grown more leeks from seed this year to obtain a bigger harvest of baby leeks in future.

As well as seed sown plants, I have raised some from the cut off ends of purchased (and eaten) leeks from the shops. They did not all take root but it can be fun to try this.

Shallots
Allium cepa aggregatum

Shallots are well known mild flavoured members of the onion family producing small bulbs that can be eaten raw or cooked. They are widely grown as annuals but are in fact hardy perennials.

Shallots are often available as sets – small bulbs which can be planted in autumn or spring. In practice they tend to be in the shops and markets in the spring, so that is the easiest time to obtain them. They should be planted about two to three centimetres deep. By the end of the growing season each bulb has divided into a number of separate bulbs which can be harvested after the tops have died back and left to dry thoroughly before storing. Conventionally the whole crop is consumed and fresh supplies purchased the following year; but I save some and replant immediately for next year's crop.

I have tried intermingling shallots with different plants and so far have found that a polyculture of shallots, Chinese artichoke and earthnut pea grows happily together.

Spring Onions
Allium cepa

I have grown a number of varieties of spring onion from seed and also planted them from bunches bought at the supermarket. Unfortunately I lost track of exactly which

Clumping spring onions; where there were two, now there are seven. (November).

Spring onion dug to check what was going on; lower part to be replanted, top part to be eaten (October).

were which in the mêlée of the garden and its rather busy polycultures but what I know is that from year to year they do survive. Some die down in autumn and re-emerge in spring resembling a clump of chives with numerous tiny leaf stalks. Others re-emerge as a single strong stem. I have just been out to see what I can see and found a plant with a strong flower head now going to seed and beside it a strong stem over 60cm long. I dug this up, ate the top part including the green top growth and replanted the bottom 1cm or so plus roots to regrow and I anticipate that it will. In future I will just cut them off at ground level and allow them to grow without the trauma of being dug up which was mainly so I could take a photograph.

These experiments lead me to postulate that perhaps any member of the onion family that likes where it lives in the garden is quite likely to be amenable to being cultivated as a perennial. This may mean smaller harvests – baby leeks rather than grown up leeks and fine green spring onion cuttings instead of fat, hot mature spring onions – but they are harvests entirely free of additional work and expense.

Annual Greens as Perennials

Whilst cogitating about onions in general it also seemed possible that perhaps some of the annual brassicas could equally be grown perennially? Also, might kales grown for their leaves be capable of living through more than one season?

Dwarf Curly Kale
Brassica oleracea acephela

I had a dwarf curly kale (that was so tiny most people would have removed it) in a less than favourable location beneath a blackcurrant bush in the shade (probably

Purple sprouting broccoli (March).

Savoy cabbage regrowing in its second year (July).

Sutherland kale in its second year (June).

nobody else would have put a kale there in the first place!). As might be expected it made very little growth yielding only minute to small amounts of leaf from time to time. The main purpose in leaving it was to see how long it would last. It died last winter of frostbite but had lived two or three years to that point. This is an experiment I will repeat again one day.

Purple Sprouting Broccoli
Brassica oleracea

Nine star perennial broccoli will live on, so might purple sprouting do the same? I have tried twice to find out only to find that the plants died during their second winter. Both times they perished after being locked in a foot deep layer of frozen snow at very sub zero temperatures for weeks. I still think it may be possible to keep them for more than one year, but clearly it will depend on winter conditions, and possibly also the variety. I will continue to try!

Savoy Cabbage
Brassica oleracea sabauda

I read about perennialising heading cabbages in the forest gardening literature. So after harvesting the cabbage heads of four Savoy cabbages I left the stalks to see what would happen. They all produced additional growth through the following season but interestingly they behaved differently from one another. One produced mini cabbage heads, one plain leaves, another produced wilder leaves than the original plant had borne and another had a mix of mini head and leaf growth. These additional harvests were less than the original heads but they were more food for no work and that is always good. The plants died in the winter of 2010-2011 and I have not repeated the experiment, but hope to someday.

Other Kales

I have also experimented with red Russian kale, Sutherland kale, 1,000 headed kale and they have all lived long enough to come to maturity, flower, set seed and continue to grow at least into the following year. Of these, 'Red Russian' kale has proved to be the longest lived. These experiments give me some confidence that many kales will happily live on from year to year providing leaves and shoots for months at a time. I have even got a Brussels sprout plant that is coming into its third summer. It doesn't bear conventional sprouts but the leaves are fine.

Other Useful Annual Greens

Some 'proper' annuals also have a use in a polyculture of perennials. The following are all very useful salad plants and will self-seed to reappear the following year with no effort on the gardener's part.

Hairy Bittercress
Cardamine hirsuta

Bitter cress was once my enemy, appearing early in the new year, growing at a tremendous pace, flowering and setting seed when I was not looking and sending the fast ripened seeds across the garden with explosive pops of the pods. Since finding out that it is edible I now welcome it! It is, as the name suggests, somewhat strong flavoured but is absolutely fine when mixed with other, milder leaves such as lamb's lettuce and claytonia.

Lamb's Lettuce
Valerianella locusta

Lamb's lettuce is a mild flavoured leaf that has been appearing and reappearing around my garden for several years now. It grows fast, appearing overnight as if from nowhere. I harvest much of the leaf growth but let the plants flower and run to seed for the next generation.

Land Cress
Barbarea verna

Land cress is a useful substitute for watercress as it has a similarly hot, peppery flavour.

Bitter cress emerging from melting snow (January).

Self sown lamb's lettuce appearing in (January).

Self sown land cress (January).

Miner's Lettuce
Claytonia perfoliata

Miner's lettuce is a mild leaf that can be grown all year round but I find it most useful as a winter salad leaf. At this time of year it is mild, but can become bitter in warm weather.

Annual Roots Grown As Perennials

If onions and greens can be perennialised to some extent why not roots? My experiment with scorzonera (Chapter Five) makes me wonder – other roots grown as annuals such as carrot, burdock, salsify and parsnip are botanically also biennial, so might they be able to be part harvested and replanted year by year?

Carrots sown in 2011 were left in the ground and many of them threw up new foliage and then flowers in the summer of 2012. The flowers were really pretty and were outstandingly attractive to insects being perpetually covered with them. They yielded masses of seed from attractive seed heads which I stored over the winter. A number of plants then made it through the harsh winter of 2012-2013 and flowered again. There were a few self-sown seedlings nearby and I have sown lots of the saved seed elsewhere. As these survivors are currently flowering I have not attempted to dig them up to see if it is tough or edible, shrunken or large. Whatever the answer to that question turns out to be I will continue to grow carrots this way, allowing the older plants to produce copious seed and then letting some of the resulting crop remain in the ground to produce yet more seed.

I have also been trying this experiment with parsnip which is at the same stage with a plant in its third summer and producing seed heads at present. Like carrots I will

The white flower in the centre is carrot in its third summer and flowering for the second time (August).

Babington's leek transplanted into a new bed by a hedge (May).

continue to grow parsnips this way. Salsify and burdock are in their first summer and I have my fingers crossed that I will find the same thing happens with them.

One thing to bear in mind with this type of experiment is that you need to use 'open pollinated' varieties not F1 hybrids. Open pollinated seeds come true to type when they are sown and grown. F1 hybrids, on the other hand, are artificially produced as the marriage of two specific varieties brought together to create plants with desired characteristics from each parent. When left in the garden to be pollinated naturally their offspring will vary from the plant you began with. F1 hybrid varieties are clearly marked on seed packets and catalogues. Old, heritage varieties will be open pollinated and at least one company, Real Seeds, only produces open pollinated seeds.

Perennials I Would Have Liked To Be Able To Grow Better

I am really sorry that I was not able to grow the following perennial vegetables successfully. Some of them I am still persisting with and others I will try again if I ever have a garden that is not damp and shady. They are all known to be reliable perennial vegetables under suitable conditions.

Babington's Leek
Allium ampeloprasum babingtonii

I have been attempting to grow Babington's leeks for five years. I think that they just do not like my garden. They begin to sprout but the leaves remain very narrow and never grow beyond a few centimetres tall. Plenty of references speak of it being an easy perennial to grow, so it must just be me. If it does succeed it will reach a height 180cm and flower in July and August.

Cardoon
Cynara cardunculus

I have grown a single cardoon plant for several years now and it reliably comes back year after year. It is a bulky plant growing up to 2m tall and extends another metre widthways. It bears attractive flowers from August to September and then lots of seeds for the birds. The stems can be earthed up early in the growing season to blanch them and remove bitterness and can then be eaten cooked or raw. Somehow I have never had time to get around to trying them but as they are sold by mainstream seed suppliers they must surely taste nice and be worth a try. In the summer my plant has been plagued by black fly, which in turn has attracted squadrons of ladybirds.

Chinese Kale
Brassica oleracea alboglabra

Chinese kale is increasingly appearing in the pages of seed catalogues as an annual but is known to be reliably perennial. It is grown primarily for its thick and tasty stems, although the young leaves and flower buds are also nice.

It is easily grown from seed and is not fussy with regard to soil and site. Mine grew strongly from seed, growing well from a sowing in April and when planted out in July they made good growth. However they quickly ran to seed in the summer sunshine and then succumbed to the predations of the cabbage white caterpillars the first year and flea beetles in the second year of experimenting.

Other growers recommend them as suitable for perennial cultivation so please do not be deterred by my lack of proficiency. The small harvest I have so far obtained was really nice and I therefore plan to continue experimenting with them to see if I can make them work.

King's Spear
Asphodeline lutea

This is a perennial plant used by the Romans for food with edible roots, young shoots and flowers. It flowers in early summer and can reach a height of 1m. I have read that it does well in sandy soils and in a warm, sunny position. I have attempted

to grow it in a non sandy soil and a not too warm and sunny position which it clearly has not liked, but it sounds appealing and I may try to offer it a nicer spot next year to see if I can succeed.

Pig Nut
Conopodium majus

This is a native British wild flower with an edible tuber. I obtained seeds and tried several sowings but did not get any to germinate. I may try again as I adore wild plants. It flowers in the summer and grows to about 30cm.

Sea Holly
Eryngium maritimum

Sea holly has edible roots and young shoots, grows up to 50cm and flowers from July to October. This is another plant that definitely did not like the place I offered it. As the name states, its natural habitat is the seashore and it clearly needs a better-drained and sunnier spot than it can have in my garden.

Sea Kale
Crambe maritima

This is a very tough plant, as it needs to be able to cope with life on the seashore – one moment drenched with salty water, the next left high and dry in the shingle. Mine happily survived the wet summer of 2009 and the following two harsh winters with no problem. My plant dies back over the winter and comes later into growth than the brassicas at the end of April. The height is 60 cm and it flowers in late spring.

Sea kale can be grown from root cuttings and from seed. Seed may need some patience – mine took a month to germinate from an outdoor sowing in March, following which they were quite slow growing.

For some people the taste is a bit strong, but if you like a hearty 'cabbagey' flavour you should like it. The young shoots and flower heads are the best eating as the older ones are stronger flavoured and tougher!

However my garden clearly does not suit it all that well and although it survives I cannot induce it to grow very much. I suspect my conditions are too damp and shady, but I will continue to move it about to see if I can find or create a better-drained and sunnier spot for it.

Certainly if you live in a coastal area, have well drained soil and sunny conditions sea kale is worth a try. When it does grow well it is massive and there will be no shortage of harvests from it! I have seen seeds and young plants available from a few nurseries; in addition to the original wild plant there is also a cultivar known as Lily White.

Tartar Bread Plant
Crambe tatarica

I was unable to get this to germinate at all. However it sounds intriguing. According to the Plants for a Future database it grows to 1m tall and has edible leaves and young stems which can be blanched, and a fleshy, sweet root, which can be eaten raw or cooked.

Miscellaneous Other Perennial Vegetables

There are some other perennial vegetables which I have tried but which did not work particularly well for me. However my experiments are focused on a small, damp and shady patch and they may well perform differently in other conditions. I would hate to do a disservice to any plant and would encourage people to experiment and draw their own conclusions.

Breadroot
Psoralea esculenta

This is a perennial root vegetable native to the USA. It grows to 30cm tall and flowers from May to July. After some years I tracked down seeds and for two summers have attempted to grow it. However it grows so slowly that I cannot determine if it will one day be useful to me or not. It may well be that the conditions here are not sufficiently similar to its native environment for it to thrive. It may just need more time.

Collards
Brassica oleracea var. *acephala*

Collards were a source of confusion for me. They seemed to be mentioned regularly in forest garden literature but impossible to obtain. It seems that there are both annual and perennial collards grown principally in the USA. I grew the annual variety with the intention of seeing if it would 'perennialise'. However no sooner were they

ea kale growing in shade (May). *Good King Henry in foreground (July).* *Lovage (July).*

beginning to grow than they flowered, ran to seed and died. I tried a couple of different types in two years and the same thing happened each time.

There is however a definite perennial variety which requires a warm climate such as the UK does not offer. I have not been able to find any way of buying it to try it out just in case.

Good King Henry
Chenopodium bonus-henricus

The young leaves and early spring shoots are edible. I tried them cooked a few times but really did not like the flavour. The plant is a mineral accumulator and birds feed on the seeds so I keep mine for these reasons. It grows to 30cm tall and is in flower from May to July.

Komatsuma / Japanese Mustard Spinach
Brassica rapa perviridis

Komatsuma is a Japanese leaf in the cabbage family which I hoped might perennialise. However it also rapidly flowered and ran to seed soon after leaving its baby pot behind.

Lovage
Levisticum officinale

Lovage can become quite a monster, so beware if you are thinking of growing it. I have seen deceptively small plants in tiny pots in the herb section at garden centres. If it likes your garden, it will grow up to 1.8m! It was because it grew too large and dominant that I decided to remove it. It is in flower in July and August.

Maximilian sunflower (July).   Perpetual spinach (June).   Tiger nut (August).

However if ample room is available it is potentially useful as a source of nectar and a sheltering place for insects.

The young leaves and stems can be eaten raw or cooked. I don't particularly care for the flavour but that is entirely personal taste.

Maximillian Sunflower
Helianthus maximiliani

This is a prairie plant, native to the United States which can reach over 2m in height. It was hard to track down and I bought mine from a flower nursery. It has been undemanding in the garden, and grew quite happily, flowering through the summer. However when I dug it up to look for tubers there were none to be seen. The Plants for a Future database does say that yields are low. Somewhat alarmingly it was showing signs of sending roots out in every direction as though it may become quite invasive. I will keep it for the moment for flowers but I am unlikely to be eating it.

Perennial Lettuce
Lactuca perennis

It sounds too good to be true, a perpetual source of one of my favourite leaves and I eventually obtained some seeds. After some trial and error they grew at the second attempt but were very small, unappetising looking plants redeemed by a lovely flower head. By the look of them they are far removed from what we now call lettuce and I have not attempted to eat them. However they have seeded themselves again in subsequent years and make an attractive flower so I am saving seed to propagate some more.

Salad Burnet
Sanguisorba minor

Young leaves and shoots are edible. I grew it but did not like the flavour. I understand it may taste better when grown on chalky soil. It is a low growing plant which may make a good ground cover and flowers through the summer.

Spinach and Sorrel
Spinacia oleracea **and** *Rumex acetosa*

I have tried a number of varieties of spinach and sorrel and left some of them in the garden for over two years to form a low ground cover. The results are mixed but on the whole they have become far too acidic to be pleasant. I wonder if the soil is so rich that the flavours are too concentrated? I am not a fan of particularly acid flavours although I know that many people love sorrel soup.

However the variety spinach 'Mediana' seems to be quite mild and I do like this one. It is reliably perennial.

Spinach 'Perpetual' / Spinach Beet
Beta vulgaris var. *vulgaris*

The seeds of perpetual spinach are widely available. It quickly turned bitter in my garden. However it may be much better behaved in other places and is worth a try. If it is not nice for eating, it will almost certainly be a mineral accumulator and can be added to the compost or used as a mulch when the time comes to remove it.

Tiger Nut
Cyperus esculentus

This is an unusual plant grown for the tuberous root which can be cooked and made into desserts and beverages as well as being dried and ground to powder. In the early 20th century they were eaten by children as confectionery.

I eventually found a supplier but the plants only grew a fraction of the 90cm they should have achieved with correspondingly tiny tubers. They need damp which I can provide, but not shady damp which is what they got. I might try again one day if conditions permit.

Borage in flower (July).

Day lily (July).

Flowers

Finally there are edible flowers to consider. I have not made much of a study of them, but have grown and eaten the flowers of day lily (*Hemerocallis*). As the name suggests these attractive flowers last only a day, so I have let them have their brief time in the sun and then picked them to eat later in the day. They are sweet and soft but with a bit of a light crunch.

Other edible flowers

- Onion family flowers, such as wild garlic, chives, garlic chives

- Asphodel

- Borage

- Campanula

- Dandelion (in fritters or wine)

- Red clover and white clover

- Violets (sometimes candied)

Harvest of winter salads, including lamb's lettuce and bittercress from the garden, with pea shoots grown indoors.

chapter 7

COOKING WITH NEW FOODS

Eating your perennial vegetables

When it's time to enjoy the fruits of your labour (or hopefully lack of labour) it helps to have some ideas. The simplest way is to use perennial vegetables as substitutes for annuals:

- Perennial kales / cabbages / leaf beet / other leaves as a cooked green vegetable side dish; I have found they are better steamed rather than boiled

- Perennial salad greens in salads in place or alongside traditional ingredients

- Perennial onions raw and cooked in place of annual onions

- Perennial roots in place of potatoes, swedes, parsnip etc

- Use whatever ingredients you have to hand to make a hearty soup

However the internet is strewn with mouth-watering recipes that can be adapted to include perennials and those below have been tested. All the recipes featured here are vegetarian and many are vegan. They are suggestions for starting points and easily varied according to what is to hand or in season.

I have a lovely book called *Wild Garlic, Gooseberries and Me* by Irish chef Denis Cotter.[*] It includes recipes using some perennials such as sea kale, Jerusalem artichoke, oca, scorzonera and is packed full of inspiration.

[*] *Wild Garlic and Gooseberries ... and me – a chef's stories and recipes from the land*; Denis Cotter; Collins, London, 2007

Hearty Chickpea and Kale Soup

Serves four to six

I first made this with a mixture of leaves from nine star perennial kale, walking stick kale and wild cabbage. All of these kale / cabbage family plants have a fairly strong taste when steamed and used plain as a green vegetable. Whilst this is no doubt indicative of their great nutritional value, the flavour may not appeal to everyone. Combining these leaves with other simple ingredients tones the flavour down and should please most palates.

This is a truly hearty soup, ideal for autumn and winter; it is lovely served with crusty bread.

For variations on the theme try:

- Changing the proportions of root vegetables
- Different beans or peas
- Varying the spices

Ingredients

Olive oil or similar for frying

250g onion, chopped

250g carrot, chopped

5 cloves garlic, finely chopped or crushed

1cm length of fresh ginger, chopped

1 x 425g can chick peas

225g (perennial) kale leaves, central stalk removed and leaves finely chopped

3 teaspoons ground cumin

1 teaspoon paprika

¼ teaspoon chilli powder or cayenne pepper or fresh / bottled equivalent

¼ teaspoon mixed spice

1 pinch saffron strands

¼ teaspoon dried cinnamon

1 litre vegetable stock

Salt if desired

Method

Begin by frying the carrots and onion in the oil until the onion begins to brown.

Add the garlic and ginger and cook for a minute.

Add the spices and cook whilst stirring for a minute.

Add the chickpeas and vegetable stock, bring to the boil then reduce the heat and simmer for twenty minutes.

Add the kale leaves and cook for ten minutes, or longer if you prefer them softer.

Taste and add salt if required or desired.

Retain some of the mixture, mostly chickpeas if you can fish them out.

Blend the remainder to your personal taste and return the retained chickpeas etc.

Dilute with more stock if you require a thinner texture.

Kale and Leek Colcannon

Serves four as an accompaniment

Ingredients

Olive oil or similar for frying

4 medium leeks, finely sliced

200g kale (perennial)

800g floury potatoes e.g. King Edward, peeled

150ml semi skimmed milk

Method

Fry the leeks in oil over a medium heat for five minutes, stirring from time to time, then add the kale and two tablespoons of water.

Season to taste, stir, turn down heat to low and cover. Leave to sweat for a further ten minutes or until both vegetables are soft. You might need to add a little more water half way through.

Meanwhile cook the potatoes in boiling water until just tender and mash with the milk until smooth.

Add the kale and leeks to the mashed potatoes, season well and mash everything together. Serve immediately.

Kale with Ginger, Garlic and Chilli

Serves two as an accompaniment

For variations on the theme try:

- Leave out the ginger and you have a perfect accompaniment for Italian dishes.
- If you're eating it with Chinese or Thai food you can add soy sauce to taste.

Ingredients

200g (perennial) kale

2cm piece of fresh ginger, peeled

4 spring onions, trimmed

2 tablespoons vegetable or nut oil

Half a red chilli, deseeded and very finely sliced

Large clove garlic, peeled and very finely sliced

Squeeze of fresh lime (optional)

Method

Place the kale into a large saucepan, cover with water and bring to the boil then simmer for four minutes.

Finely chop the ginger and cut the spring onions into lengths, about 3cm, slicing on the diagonal.

Drain the kale really well and heat the oil in a large frying pan or wok.

Add the chilli, garlic, ginger and spring onions and cook over a medium heat for two minutes, ensuring garlic remains pale in colour.

Add the drained kale into the pan and combine it with the remaining ingredients (apart from the lime).

Cook for about one and a half minutes, constantly tossing the kale to heat it through This will also allow it to take on the flavours of the other ingredients.

Season to taste, add a squeeze of fresh lime and serve immediately.

Wild Rocket Soup

The flavour of wild rocket is very peppery and possibly too hot for most people unless blended with some other milder ingredients for example this satisfyingly smooth and soothing soup. Wild rocket will grow year round so this can be made at any time of year but on cool, misty autumn or cold fresh winter days it may seem particularly appropriate to the mood.

Ingredients

15ml olive oil

1 small onion chopped

2 large cloves garlic chopped

1 medium eating apple chopped

350g potatoes chopped

75-100g rocket leaves (weight after removing from stalks)

600ml vegetable stock

Method

Sauté the onion and garlic for five minutes in the olive oil.

Add the potatoes, apple, wild rocket and stock, bring to the boil, turn the heat down and simmer for 10 minutes or until the potatoes are cooked.

Blend the mixture until smooth.

Add salt and or pepper to taste and garnish if you feel artistic!

Roasted Perennial Root Vegetables

Ingredients

Mixture of root vegetables as available including: Jerusalem artichoke, mashua, oca, skirret, yacon, yam. Washed or peeled and chopped into large chunks.

Garlic according to taste

Onions

Salt and pepper to taste

Olive oil as required

Method

Mix all ingredients together and roast in a hot oven until tender but not overcooked.

Flowery edge to the polyculture including three cornered leek, Welsh onion, self-seeded columbine and forget me nots (June).

chapter 8

PLANTS TO COMPLETE A POLYCULTURE

By letting go of preconceived ideas about the disadvantages of some familiar plants they can be turned to good if somewhat unfamiliar uses.

Plants that accumulate minerals, confuse pests and supply nectar are required to complete a polyculture, some of the many options are detailed below. There are familiar plants put to unfamiliar uses including some regarded as 'weeds' or downright nuisances. However even those that have a poor reputation have positive attributes and if correctly managed can be valuable to a polyculture.

In practice I have considered my entire garden to be one large polyculture. This means that some of the functions such as accumulating minerals can be done by plants outside the actual vegetable patches. It only involves a small amount of work to transfer some harvested leaves of nettle or comfrey to the vegetable patch. Other functions such as confusing pests and fixing nitrogen are needed close to the vegetables themselves.

I have divided these plants up according to the layer that they occupy, from tall to low and then climbers.

Tall Plants

Name	Uses	Notes
Chicory *Cichorium intybus*	Accumulates minerals Attracts insects	Chicory is a deep-rooted mineral accumulator often mentioned as a useful plant to have in a forest garden. If it is planted in a smaller area such as a back garden polyculture vegetable patch, it needs to be watched. Mine grew very rapidly in the second summer and neighbouring plants appeared to be suffering as a result. Once I had cut the chicory back to more modest proportions a better balance was established.
Comfrey *Symphytum officinale*	Accumulates minerals Attracts insects	Comfrey has become well known as a plant to use for fertilising an organic garden. It can be invasive and seed itself around readily, if this is likely to be a nuisance choose the 'Bocking 14' strain of Russian comfrey which does not set seed. I have it growing in the hedges and edges rather than in with the vegetables.
Fennel *Foeniculum vulgare*	Attracts insects Confuses pests Medicinal and culinary herb	Fennel is a familiar and very attractive herb which comes in either green or bronze colour. With stately stems swaying in the summer breeze and uncountable numbers of insects adorning the flowers and the aniseed of its fragrance, it is a lovely plant in any garden and particularly valuable in a polyculture. I do not know yet if it is coincidence, but when the brassicas were badly attacked by caterpillars the plants close by the fennel were less badly affected than most of the others. I allow some fennel plants to self-seed in the vegetable patch, but not too many.
Foxglove *Digitalis* species	Attracts insects	The foxglove is particularly useful in shady areas. It will self-seed and provide flowers attractive to insects and people alike. I don't have them in with the vegetables, but they grow happily on the edges of the garden. This plant is very toxic if eaten.

Name	Uses	Notes
Rosebay willowherb *Epilobium angustifolium*	Accumulates minerals Attracts insects	Rosebay willowherb is definitely unpopular and you do have to be careful with it; I would not, for example, let it flower and set seed. However as a mineral accumulator it is unsurpassed, as far as I can establish. Compared to chicory (which is itself a respectable mineral accumulator) it contains four times the calcium, twice the iron, five times the magnesium, twice the phosphorus, slightly more potassium, five times the zinc, slightly more copper, fifteen times the manganese and three times the selenium.* This means rosebay willowherb can potentially be very useful. However, being this able to accumulate nutrients may mean that it can take them away from other plants and I have only used it when it has appeared on the wilder fringes of my garden, cutting it back and using the cuttings for green mulch where needed.

* Source: U.S. Department of Agriculture, Agricultural Research Service. 2011. USDA National Nutrient Database for Standard Reference, Release 24. Nutrient Data Laboratory Home Page, www.ars.usda.gov/ba/bhnrc/ndl

Fennel flower adorned by eight hoverflies (August).

Rosebay willowherb appearing alongside three cornered leek in a new bed (May).

Medium Height Plants

Name	Uses	Notes
Dock *Rumex* species	Accumulates minerals	I have allowed dock plants to remain on the wilder edges of the garden, pulling leaves off regularly to prevent them getting too large and using the leaves for green mulch where needed. They do not spread around as my no dig policy means there is no undisturbed soil for them to colonise. Never let them flower or set seed.
Horseradish *Amoracia rusticana*	Accumulates minerals Confuses pests	Culinary herb. Horseradish has a deep taproot which enables it to accumulate minerals from deep in the soil. Its strong smell also acts as a pest confuser and of course it is traditionally used for horseradish sauce. It is best used fresh rather than stored. Dig up the root, which will probably break leaving you with the top portion; the plant will regrow from the remaining root.
Lemon balm *Melissa officinalis*	Confuses pests Accumulates minerals Attracts insects Can be used for teas	Lemon balm is a well-known garden herb which is undemanding and easy to grow. I have planted a few close to perennial brassicas. Self-seeds everywhere.
Mint *Mentha* species	Confuses pests Attracts insects	Culinary herb. Mints suffer from a mixed reputation. Whilst useful for tea and for cooking, confusing pests and attracting beneficial insects, its tendency to spread itself about means that it needs to be used with care. I break or cut the stems down hard when they reach about 10cm. This takes the vigour out of them and stops them spreading too much. I have planted some mints with the perennial greens.

Horseradish front in new polyculture (July).   *Lemon balm in autumn sun (November).*   *Large clump of sweet cicely in flower (June).*

Name	Uses	Notes
Stinging nettle *Urtica dioica*	Accumulates minerals Edible leaves Attracts insects	Just in case you missed them in Chapter Five – I would not be without nettles! Their rapid growth – which I cut back regularly to below the level of surrounding plants – provides ample mulch material throughout the growing season. Their soft foliage blends well with the stronger, stiffer forms of perennial kales. I allow them to grow where they will on the wilder edges of the garden and harvest them periodically for mulch on the vegetable patches.
Sweet Cicely *Myrrhis odorata*	Confuses pests Attracts insects Culinary herb	Sweet cicely loves woodland or similarly shady situations. It is covered with a mass of attractive white flowers early in spring and is also a pest confuser. The leaves can be used when cooking tart fruits like gooseberries to sweeten them. This is a lovely plant but needs to be kept in check. In my garden it tends to proliferate and I remove young plants while I can. Left alone they get large and swamp their neighbours. It is probably best confined to the hedges and edges and not allowed in the vegetable patch itself.
Wild Marjoram *Oreganum vulgare*	Confuses pests Attracts insects Culinary herb	Marjoram flowers are adored by bees and other insects and are continually smothered with them all summer. It readily self-seeds but I can't get enough because of its outstanding attractiveness to insects.

Ground Cover and Low Plants

Ground covers shade the soil and prevent some evaporation; their physical presence also prevents other plants you definitely do not want from growing. They can be chosen for many different reasons and functions aside from their primary role. People who like more order may prefer plants with a defined habit like thymes, violets or wild strawberries.

Name	Uses	Notes
Bee balm *Monarda* species	Attracts insects Medicinal herb Herbal tea	Bee balm speaks for itself, bees adore it. I have tried both wild and cultivated forms and my garden is happier with the latter which is very attractive.
Clover *Trifolium* species	Nitrogen fixers Attract insects	There are a number of different clovers of which I have tried two. I have learned to be wary of white clover (*Trifolium repens*) as it has taken to charging around the garden swamping anything in its path and I am in the process of removing it. It is probably all right in a forest garden with trees for competition but I cannot allow it in the vegetable patch. By contrast I have a pink clover grown from a pack of sprouting seeds which forms single plants without runners. It looks attractive, the bees love it and it sits there quietly fixing nitrogen for the patch. Unfortunately, I don't know the name of the variety.
Creeping Jenny *Lysimachia nummularia*	Attracts insects	This has always been in the garden. It wanders around, looking attractive, but is easy to pull up if in the way.
Dandelion *Taraxacum officinale*	Accumulates minerals Attracts insects Medicinal herb	Dandelion is the bane of many gardeners, but I would contend that its advantages outweigh its disadvantages, particularly when grown in a no dig system which seems to prevent it from seeding everywhere. Dandelions have attractive blooms (when looked at without prejudice) giving early colour in the spring, plentiful leaves full of nutrients to use for mulch and eventually seed heads which attract goldfinches to my garden.

Name	Uses	Notes
Feverfew *Tanacetum parthenium*	Attracts insects Medicinal herb	Low growing with tiny white daisy like flowers. Can self-seed a lot if it likes the garden.
Thyme *Thymus* species	Confuses pests Attracts insects Culinary herb Ground cover	Thyme is of course another very familiar culinary herb and there are many lovely varieties to choose from.
Violet *Viola* species	Edible leaves and flowers Ground cover	Dog violet is widespread in my garden, particularly in the damper, shadier corners. It makes a lovely ground cover plant, flowers early in spring and has edible leaves and flowers which make an attractive addition to salads. Other plants in the viola family are likely to be equally lovely and amenable.
Wild strawberry *Fragaria* species	Edible fruits Ground cover Medicinal herb	Wild strawberries are also widespread in my garden, and if they were not I would introduce them. They bloom from early in the year well into the autumn and produce delectable sweet fruits for months on end. They will grow in poor soil close to rocks and on the edge of paths and in shady places under trees or other foliage. When they get an opportunity to grow in rich soil in sunshine the plants and their fruits grow correspondingly larger. I do not know which variety I have but it does not produce runners so it is easily managed. Clearly they are technically not vegetables but they fit extremely well in a perennial vegetable patch.
Yarrow *Achillea millefolium*	Confuses pests Attracts insects Accumulates minerals Medicinal herb	There are many cultivated forms of yarrow as well as the wild plant. I have used them both, they are very attractive and the wild plant in particular attracts lots of insects.

Dandelion seed heads throughout the front garden polyculture (May).

Lemon thyme on the edge of the polyculture (June).

Wild strawberry (June).

A cultivated variety of yarrow, centre (June).

Ivy in flower (November).

Golden hops growing through black elder tree with sweet cicely beneath (July).

Peas growing in centre of polyculture between second year parsnip on left and mashua on right (July).

Climbers

In a polyculture of perennial vegetables there may or may not be a place for climbing plants, but I have included a few here for the sake of completeness.

Name	Uses	Notes
Cleavers *Galium aparine*	Accumulates minerals	This is another unpopular plant with gardeners, but I like to let it scramble up the hedges and fences in late spring. It is easily pulled off and I just drop it to the ground or fold it up and place it round plants I want to feed. If left unchecked it can strangle plants or cause them to collapse, so if you have it in the garden, keep an eye on it.

(continues overleaf)

Name	Uses	Notes
Grape *Vitis* species	Accumulates minerals	I have a small grape vine grown from a seed that has been in the garden from before I began this project. I was not that excited about it as it has never flowered and probably never will, but then I found details of the mineral content of grape leaves. Again, when compared to the mineral content of chicory they have more than three times the calcium, nearly three times the iron, three times the magnesium, about half the potassium, one and a half times the zinc, nearly one and a half times the copper, over six times the manganese and three times the selenium,* thus making it a very useful addition to the garden. My grape grows up a wall dividing two of the vegetable patches in the front and back gardens and seems to be happy there without causing a problem. If I was planting it again I might choose a place away from the vegetables just in case it took too many nutrients directly from them.
Hop *Humulus lupulus*	Edible including use as a tea and in beer Medicinal herb	I already had a golden hop growing in the garden before starting out with perennial vegetables. It makes prolific growth up through a large greengage tree through the summer and I happily haul it down in the autumn and use it for a green mulch. It makes so much growth that it must contribute a significant amount of nutrients back to the garden.
Ivy *Hedera helix*	Attracts insects	Ivy is so commonplace that it is easy to miss or dismiss it but it is invaluable to wildlife, especially the berries which come later than those on many other plants. It can become a nuisance if unchecked, but a certain amount is very useful in a forest garden or just growing up a fence or tree in any garden.

* Source: U.S. Department of Agriculture, Agricultural Research Service. 2011. USDA National Nutrient Database for Standard Reference, Release 24. Nutrient Data Laboratory Home Page, www.ars.usda.gov/ba/bhnrc/ndl

Nitrogen fixers

Whilst there are various perennial nitrogen fixing trees, shrubs and plants available and suitable for a forest garden, the reduced scale of a perennial vegetable patch is easily dominated by a fast growing and powerful nitrogen-fixing thug. For a perennial vegetable patch one of the clovers, a root such as ground nut (*Apios americana*) and earth nut pea (*Lathyrus tuberosus*) are about the limit of the perennial choices that I am aware of.

I am increasingly favouring annual nitrogen fixers – peas, beans and vetches – and have been incorporating these for several years now. Allowing them to produce pods and beans or peas will focus their nitrogen fixing ability on this task and it is necessary to use judgement based on observation as to whether the garden needs the nitrogen more than you need or want the beans and peas. It is not a scientific observation, but an anecdotal one, but leaving beans and peas to produce pods does not seem to diminish the fertility of my garden. If it looked like it might I would remove the young pods.

I have grown various varieties of runner bean, Trail of Tears French bean, broad beans, field beans, varieties of mangetout and garden peas, and lots of marrowfat peas direct from supermarket packs. In the last year I have added wild vetch seeds as they are so attractive in flower.

Sometimes field beans (which are sold as a green manure) and broad beans have survived through the winter from an autumn sowing, sometimes severe weather has killed them, despite my attempts I have not been able to keep any individual plant for as much as a year, never mind more. I tend to save seed from beans and peas from year to year so once I have grown a variety I have an assured future supply.

Flowers

The garden would not be complete without some flowers! I try to have something flowering for as many months as possible, so spring bulbs give way to lots of different flowers planted in pots and beds where they can be enjoyed from the house. My favourites are the penstemmons and purpletop vervain (*Verbena bonariensis*), but there are also geums, primulas, roses, winter jasmine, forsythia and lots of others. However my overall favourites are the wild flowers which include toadflax, self heal, wild violet, primrose, cowslip, oxlip, herb Robert, wood anemone, teasel and evening primrose.

Fennel, Jerusalem artichoke and clover in centre, oca, clover and young yacon in foreground (July).

chapter 9

PATHWAYS TO POLYCULTURE

*Thinking things through in advance focuses the intention
and helps prevent making obvious mistakes.*

Starting points and general principles

It is more than likely that you already have 'polycultures' of flowers in your garden, and unless you are a professional gardener or designer, that has evolved in a somewhat haphazard fashion over time as you acquired and tried new plants. My early vegetable polycultures were meticulously planned in advance; but as tends to happen with even the best of plans they did not always work out as intended. I began to relax a bit and allow things to unfold of their own accord a bit more.

However although the plans altered over time, I am convinced that thinking things through in advance focuses the attention and intention. It also gives a structure to thoughts, concepts and ideas against which it is possible to measure or assess what actually happens. It can also help prevent making obvious mistakes. I could have stuck rigidly to my plans, but that would have left gaps in places where some plants failed to make it and I would probably not have been able to accommodate new plants I wanted to try. These general principles and guidelines are intended to help you decide on the form and composition of a perennial vegetable polyculture.

Most of what I have read of polycultures is based on selecting two or three vegetables that have complementary forms and functions that can be inter-planted in a semi structured and repeatable way and using this 'pattern' to plant a (small or large) area with that combination. I may well have adopted this approach if I had more space to play with, but in many cases I have only had room to try one or two plants of the fifty plus vegetables I have tested. Thus the experimental polycultures have comprised an evolving blend of plants sharing the same patch of ground.

The size, shape and habit of perennial roots, leafy greens and oniony vegetables indicates that they may prefer to grow in their own themed groups or clusters with a range of other supporting plants around them.

Perennial roots and tubers as a group tend to produce either bulky or tall plants and obviously the ground has to be disturbed to harvest and replant. It is therefore impractical to place them too near plants that would dislike the close presence of hungry neighbours, the shade they give or the disturbance when they are dug. Roots and tubers combine happily with suitable wild plants. I have nettles by vigorous growers like Jerusalem artichoke and wild strawberries, wild violets, forget-me-nots, self heal, herb Robert and pink clover running amongst other roots. Alternatively self-seeding annuals like lamb's lettuce and claytonia could cope with the disruption, or nitrogen fixers or other green manures might keep sleeping roots company over the winter months.

The brassica family tend to form large, stiff plants. If they are in the shade or crowded they start to lean and possibly topple. They need high fertility and are also perhaps the most likely of all the perennial vegetables to succumb to pests. I have found that under planting with a ground cover, of thyme for example, and encircling them with soft leaved, medium height herbaceous perennials like lemon balm and nettles allows them room to grow and some protection from pests like the cabbage white which apparently locates cabbages visually.

Other leafy perennials have their own quirks to be taken into account. Once wild rocket gets going it sprawls and leans everywhere. Buckler leaved sorrel likewise is a busy plant and produces masses of exquisitely pretty growth; whereas other sorrels have a more confined upright habit and can get hidden.

Initially I placed members of the onion family in amongst the other greens to maximise their use as aromatic pest confusers. However their slender erect stems tended to flop over or become swamped by more vigorous and larger neighbours as the season progressed. They can still grow, but seemingly not to their full advantage and are harder to spot when looking for harvests. I therefore now prefer to grow them away from the brassicas when possible, nestling amongst low ground cover plants.

Planning a polyculture

At first this can seem a bit daunting, like creating a living, three dimensional jigsaw puzzle. Planning how to include some of the unfamiliar plants and cater for all the elements of polyculture does not have to be too complicated, indeed I strongly recommend starting simply.

The table below lists four perennial greens, onions and roots which could provide a starting point, plus a number of other plants that fulfil other functions. The examples use plants ranging from small to tall to add variety of structure and form and provide different niches for wildlife and insects. They are specific to a home garden scale but equally may apply to edge plantings in a forest garden. Any or all of them can easily be substituted with similar perennial (or annual) vegetables as detailed in Chapters Five and Six.

Creating Edible Polycultures

Tall	Medium	Low	Notes
Perennial Greens			
Asparagus			Beautiful foliage
	Nine star perennial broccoli		Stocky plant
		Wild beet	Very hardy
		Wild rocket	Flowers attract insects
Perennial Onions			
		Chives	Flowers attract insects
		Shallots	Normally annual, can be grown perennially
		Tree onion	Reproduces from bulbils
	Welsh onion		Very hardy

Tall	Medium	Low	Notes

Roots and Tubers

Tall	Medium	Low	Notes
		Chinese artichoke	Spreads by runners
Jerusalem artichoke			Flowers attract insects
	Oca		Bulky, sprawling plants
Skirret			Flowers attract insects

Other Plants to Support a Polyculture

Tall	Medium	Low	Notes
		Creeping Jenny	Ground cover with attractive flowers through the summer
		Dandelion	Excellent mineral accumulator, flowers attract insects early in spring, seeds for finches
Fennel			Flowers attract masses of insects, aromatic pest confuser, self-seeds, culinary and medicinal herb, attractive flowers and foliage
	Lemon balm		Aromatic pest confuser
	Nettles		Young leaves edible, insect habitat, excellent mineral accumulator
		Pink clover	Nitrogen fixer, attracts insects
		Thyme	Ground cover, aromatic pest confuser, flowers attract insects also culinary and medicinal herb

	Wild marjoram	Aromatic pest confuser, attracts insects galore for months, herb
	Wild strawberry	Ground cover, attract insects, flower and fruit from spring to autumn
	Wild violet	Ground cover, attractive early spring flowers for bees
	Yarrow	Flowers attract insects, mineral accumulator, medicinal herb

If you enjoy making paper plans you could draw a (scale) diagram of the polyculture patch and populate the diagram with the plants you choose before venturing out to plant them. Alternatively you can play around with different arrangements at planting time. If you prefer not to plant in polycultures, individual perennial vegetables can be tried out in the annual vegetable patch or in the flower border or any other place you like.

It is a matter of individual preference, local conditions and the availability of different plants as to how many to include in your polyculture. However my experiments with so many new and unusual vegetables in a relatively short space of time, leads me to the conclusion that it may be best not to start out with more species than you are likely to be able to cope with. It is disappointing when seedlings and young plants die for lack of sufficient time to watch and nurture them. However, enthusiasm and optimism are wonderful traits so if you want to be ambitious in your initial plans go ahead!

Size and scale

As my space for polycultures is small my experience is by definition based on managing small areas. I don't think it is necessarily more difficult or complicated to grow polycultures in a larger space, particularly after a year or two of experience. As the plants will be moved or changed relatively infrequently it is important to remember the principle of maintaining as much diversity as possible. Many of the plants included in this book will work well in a forest garden.

Polycultures in pots, mixtures of Welsh onion with leafy greens in front, oca and Trail of Tears beans behind (July).

SITE SELECTION AND PREPARATION

Perennial vegetables will be with you for a long time and it is best to ensure they are healthy and going into well prepared ground.

Where to grow perennial vegetables

I am sure perennial vegetables can be incorporated into any method of cultivation, whether that be polycultures or more traditional arrangements, either incorporated into a permaculture design or a more standard vegetable plot. They are eminently suited to growing in forest gardens. I also think that gardeners with allotments, community gardens or participating in land sharing arrangements may find perennials very useful in terms of reducing the maintenance and overall work load.

They are in general hardy and tolerant plants that can withstand tougher conditions than annual vegetables. Therefore the choice of where to grow perennial vegetables comes down to what suits individual circumstances.

My experimental polycultures have spread by degrees round the garden from the only patch with any reliable sun, to shady and unlikely places where almost nothing of any interest would previously grow, still less anything edible. These experimental polycultures indicate that resilient perennial vegetables can take advantage of sites which are unsuitable for conventional annual vegetables. Ultimately this may prove to be a good way of making the best use of some parcels of land and I do not hesitate to try them out anywhere. My latest experiment (in a new garden) is a 'hedgetable patch' of perennial vegetables growing alongside a large established boundary hedge. It was an invention born of necessity at the time, but looks like it is working well. So don't despair if you don't have an apparently suitable place, just try what you have.

Site preparation and initial fertility

Unless the chosen site is already being used on a 'no dig' basis it may need to be dug initially to remove weeds or other unwanted plants and break up any compacted layers. Any good general gardening or permaculture book will give very full details of how to do this.

As described in chapter one my early polycultures began with planting into ground that was already in cultivation for either shrubs or annual vegetables. As things have progressed I have begun new polycultures from scratch in other parts of the garden and have adopted a very simple method for these:

- To dig up an area of lawn, overturn the turf and mulch on top with lots of organic matter.

- Or to take turf removed from elsewhere in the garden and place it directly onto lawn that is too hard to dig up, then mulch with lots of organic matter.

- Organic matter has been anything that is available – grass cuttings, hedge trimmings, compost, twigs and sticks, leaf mould, shredded paper etc.

This is in effect a version of the technique of 'sheet mulching,' which is known to be a very effective way of building a soil quickly on virgin ground. *Gaia's Garden*[*] by Toby Hemenway and *Perennial Vegetables*[†] by Eric Toensmeier give clear accounts of how to lay a good sheet mulch.

If you do begin by digging, it is important to bear in mind, that (as described in Chapter Three) fertility is quickly lost when land is cleared of plants. It is therefore extremely important to do something to ease this loss, either by planting your intended crops immediately, planting a green manure or covering the land with mulch. Planting has the advantage of continuing to maintain a live soil food web, mulching will at least feed the decomposer food web.

Ideally the next stage is to sow a green manure, but if you have plants that need a home then you may need to get them in first and perhaps sow a green manure round them. Green manures are fast growing crops which help to break up the soil. They are cut down, usually before flowering, and dug in to add nutrients to the soil. After this the intended crops can be planted. The table below gives details of some

[*] *Gaia's Garden, a Guide to Home-Scale Permaculture*; Toby Hemenway; Chelsea Green Publishing Company, Vermont, 2000
[†] *Perennial Vegetables*; Eric Toensmeier; Chelsea Green Publishing Company, Vermont, 2007

Decking removed from the centre ground and lawn removed from foreground, both areas covered with upturned turf and then copious amounts of compost (April).

Green manures two months later – mustard starting to flower in foreground, remainder of patch is phacelia (June).

green manures and when to sow them and turn them in. There is a wide choice of both annuals and perennials that are suited to a range of soil conditions and can be started from spring to autumn. Some fix nitrogen; others have exceptionally deep roots for breaking up compacted soils. If the project might take some time to get going then a perennial might be a safe bet as it can always be dug in sooner if things go faster than planned! If it is not going to be long before the main plants are ready for sowing an annual species will be fine.

Green manure	Description	Soil conditions	Sow	Turn in
Alfalfa (perennial)	Tall Very deep roots Nitrogen fixer	Most soils, not acid or waterlogged, drought resistant	Spring to summer	Summer to autumn or later, can be left for up to two years
Red clover	Medium Deep roots Nitrogen fixer	Good loam	Spring to summer	Summer to autumn or later, turn in before flowering
White clover	Low Average roots Nitrogen fixer	Most soils	Late winter to summer	Summer to autumn or later, I would advise caution as it can get very vigorous

Green manure	Description	Soil conditions	Sow	Turn in
Trefoil	Low Average roots Nitrogen fixer	Most soils including light and dry, not acid	Late spring to summer	Summer or any time as required. Will grow for up to two seasons. Tolerates semi shade and can be under sown beneath other plants
Buckwheat	Deep roots	Will grow in poor soils	Spring to summer	Summer to autumn
Crimson clover	Medium Average roots Nitrogen fixer	Prefers sandy loam, but tolerates heavy clay	Spring to summer	Summer to autumn
Fenugreek	Average roots	Heavy to light soils, prefers good drainage	Spring Summer	Summer Autumn
Annual lupin	Low Very deep roots Nitrogen fixer	Best for light, slightly acid soil	Spring	Early summer Summer / before flowering
Mustard	Low Average roots	Reasonably fertile with some moisture	Late spring Summer Early autumn	Summer Autumn Late autumn / before flowering
Phacelia	Medium Average roots	Most soils	Late spring to early autumn	Summer to late autumn / before flowering
Tares	Average roots	Heavier soils best. Does not like light or acid soils	July to September	Autumn to winter / before flowering
Field beans	Medium height Average roots	Loam to heavy clay, not drought tolerant	Autumn	Spring

Establishing the patch and ongoing fertility

Depending on personal priorities and choices it can take some time to accumulate the perennial vegetables that will ultimately form the main part of the planting. Be aware of letting enthusiasm take over and launching into planting young plants out too soon! Perennial vegetables will be with you for a long time and it is best to ensure they are healthy and going into well-prepared ground. The table below details the general tasks that can be undertaken through the seasons.

Spring March to May	Summer June to August	Autumn September to November	Winter December to February
Planning	Planning	Planning	Planning
Build fertility by planting green manure or mulching or both	Build fertility by planting green manure or mulching or both	Build fertility by planting green manure or mulching or both	Build fertility using mulch
Begin to sow seeds when weather warms	Sow seeds Plant out spring sown seedlings if large enough	Plant out spring or summer sown seedlings if large enough	
	Plant purchased plants or tubers	Plant purchased plants or tubers	

It takes time for some perennial vegetables to establish. Plants grown from seed or from small tubers can take over a year to mature.

The possibility of growing robust, nutritious and healthy vegetables in some unlikely places in my garden has been due entirely to building a deep and fertile soil, rich in micro and not so microorganisms. I am not a soil scientist (any more than any other kind of expert), but it seems to me that getting organic matter into the soil is the simplest way of achieving this. Over the years of experimenting I have not dug at all, yet I have a soil that is sweet smelling, retains moisture well and grows some absurdly large plants. In some places it is also really very light and almost fluffy. On one occasion I intended to pull a few dandelion and dock leaves to use for mulch but the soil was so soft and light that the entire plants came out in my hand, with even their minor roots intact.

Dandelions and a dock plant came out of the ground intact with a gentle tug (May).

A mulch of cut up chicory leaves is laid behind the Asturian tree cabbage. Right of the oca and kale the mulch is comprised of cut up prunings from trees and shrubs and unwanted greenery removed from the patch (July).

My approach to mulch has however been somewhat haphazard. If I had known from the outset that I would be writing about it I may have been a little more organized and prescriptive. However what I have done has worked very well so I continue in the same fashion. The original polyculture patch was frequently loaded with the not entirely decomposed contents of the compost bin, often in order to make room for more wastes to go into the bin. I endeavoured to rescue most of the obviously not quite decomposed bits like eggshells, orange peel, corn cobs (I know some people don't put some things that take longer into the compost) to put back in the bin, but I have been in trouble on occasion for allowing the garden to look unsightly. In my defence this was always in winter when we were not outside and could not see the offending articles.

To the partially composted mulch, prunings from shrubs and even small branches have been added as they have been generated. I have stood in a frozen solid garden in January cutting woody materials into 10-20cm lengths with a pair of secateurs wondering if the massive piles I made could possibly disappear by spring or even the summer. But it really is amazing how much material like this that a garden can 'eat'. Sometimes when spring arrived some of the residue of this mulch remained, but the growing plants soon hid it. Having started this way I continue to use anything that comes to hand for mulch.

More orthodox mulch can be made from fully decomposed homemade compost on its own or with other materials such as straw, hay, leaves and wood chips. I only ever lay things on the soil surface as I am pretty sure that this draws the worms and other creatures up to see what is there and to do their thing. I understand that it is important that dry or woody materials are left on the surface and not dug in.

Digging them in feeds the decomposer organisms below ground and leads to population explosions. The end result of this is that valuable nitrogen is taken up by the soil life and becomes unavailable to plants.

Raising plants from seed

I am definitely no expert in this but my mistakes have taught me well and have led to this guidance:

- Take note of and follow closely the instructions on seed packets.

- Use good peat free, organic seed compost.

- Label pots and trays meticulously, do not try to remember what is what.

- Try to avoid getting carried away and sowing more seeds than you are likely to be able to manage.

- Watch the pots daily for germination and to ensure that they don't dry out or get waterlogged.

- Read a conventional gardening book or website about seed sowing techniques.

- Raise plants in pots or appropriate sized trays; do not plant direct into the seedbed unless you are sure that your precious seedlings won't get eaten.

Deciding when to plant out needs to be quite carefully judged. On the one hand plants need to be healthy and robust, particularly members of the cabbage family that are susceptible to slugs. On the other hand, if left too long confined in a pot they will have grown too large and will become stunted and stop growing. It is as well to leave the cabbage family plants in good sized pots (I use 454g yogurt pots) until the main stem starts to thicken up and become a bit less juicy. However be aware that cabbages and kales are hungry plants and will stop growing if kept too long confined in a pot they have grown too large for. When they are sufficiently mature pop plants into the ground according to the prepared plan and water well. If there is no prepared plan, then pop them in and watch particularly closely what happens.

It is best to observe the spacing given on the seed packet or to ensure sufficient space so that when they reach their mature size that plants won't be crowding each other out. I have been guilty of squashing my poor plants in far too close together to begin with, in part so that I could try out as many varieties as possible, but I am sure that they suffered as a result. I have now moved them round and removed a few to ensure that they each have adequate room.

If space is limited some of the plants for other functions in a polyculture may have to go in a separate part of the garden. For instance comfrey or other mineral accumulators can be grown in a separate patch and used to mulch around the vegetable patch as needed. It might mean a bit more work, but ultimately all the benefit derived from the garden will be retained within it. By the same token it is not absolutely necessary to site the nectar plants within the patch; they can equally well be placed in a near or adjacent part of the garden.

It is more than likely that young plants will be ready to plant out at different times. If a green manure has been planted and turned in and all systems are go for getting the polyculture started, there are a few options for how to organise a staggered planting without compromising the ideal of keeping the soil continuously planted if at all possible.

- Plants that comprise the supporting cast such as lemon balm, thyme, dandelion, yarrow, nettles are often more readily available than the perennial vegetables. You can begin the site with planting these and allowing them to develop into a welcoming carpet awaiting the arrival of the vegetables.

- When some plants are ready and others are not, plant more of those that are ready, using the space designated for the others. When the latter are ready, remove some of the early plants and pop the others in. Those removed could be put in another part of the garden, given to a friend or perhaps eaten!

- Sow or plant something else to take care of the spare space for a while. Maybe some ground cover plants or another green manure.

- Cover the ground with mulch or homemade compost.

- If you are brave or short of time leave things and see what grows, but do pay attention to what happens.

Fruit trees, bushes and forest gardens

My garden is also home to a venerable old greengage tree, two pear trees, three apple trees, raspberries, blackcurrants, blackberries, strawberries, wild strawberries, gooseberry, jostaberry, buffalo berry, tayberry and a wineberry. I have not mentioned fruit in particular but where the vegetable polycultures come up against the assorted fruits they intermingle very happily.

Potted polycultures

I am aware that many people don't have even the luxury of a small patch of ground and need to grow their vegetables in pots. I have done a little experimenting with perennials in pots and found so far that pots work better for onions and roots than for greens. Perennial greens are hungry plants and those in pots were pale imitations of the garden grown plants. Some of the plants / combinations that seemed to like growing together this summer were:

- Oca with Trail of Tears beans (only the oca is perennial in this combination)
- Oca with earth nut pea
- Welsh onions with annual salad greens
- Yam with Trail of Tears bean

This is anecdotal and just an indication of what might work for you. It is probably worth experimenting with different combinations of perennial roots and beans or perennial onions and beans. One thing I noticed was that the deeper the pot or bag the stronger the plants grew.

Storing produce

A bumper harvest means that you may need to store your produce for some time. Tubers such as yacon, Jerusalem artichoke, oca, mashua need cool, dry, dark and airy conditions as warmth, damp and light can start off rots or premature bursting into growth. In some winters my garage easily supplies suitable conditions, other times it is too cold or damp. Perhaps ideally they would like a cool, airy cupboard but we don't have one so they can get moved around a bit.

Another possibility is pickling your produce. I have read and been fascinated by Sandor Katz's book *Wild Fermentation*[*] which includes a diverse range of preserving methods for different foods. I have not had a go yet but I do fancy attempting to make kimchi to preserve both leafy and root vegetables.

[*] *Wild Fermentation – the flavor, nutrition and craft of live-culture foods*; Sandor Ellix Katz; Chelsea Green Publishing Company, 2003

*Keeping the bees
happy with clover.*

chapter 11

'MANAGING' A POLYCULTURE

Participating with nature instead of seeking to control her becomes an integral part of our own nature and the realisation dawns that this is a true path to sustainability.

If they were left completely alone most gardens in the UK (and other similar wet, temperate climates) would revert to woodland which is nature's ultimate conclusion on what should be growing there. Most gardening is an attempt to interrupt and control or guide nature with forest gardening being a notable exception. The more I journey along this road of polyculture the more daft it seems to try to intervene and dictate to nature what I want to grow (or not to grow) in a certain place.

Here I am suggesting guidelines, not rules. One day you may realise that you have grown so in touch with your patch and how nature is operating in it that actions are intuitive. You get hunches and inspirations and start branching out with new ideas; this is ultimately the best way of 'managing' a polyculture. Maybe by describing it I can bring out a flavour of this wildness that works and help provide a guide to becoming a collaborator with the garden rather than its boss.

On balance

Differences between gardeners as individuals become evident through the variations in their gardens. One person's paradise is another's jungle. Conversely a picture perfect plot may seem over precise or fussy to someone else. In our own gardens we can decide what we like and as much of conventional gardening is about exerting control that is what many gardeners have learned to do. However growing polycultures means refocussing on maintaining balance. The aim is to learn how to nudge nature in the desired direction; but this is not learned over night and nor from a book. However I will attempt to describe how I have become acquainted with balance.

In spring the Daubenton's kales are cradled first in a cloud of forget-me-nots and then embraced by young nettles. The nine star perennials are similarly held gently by a cluster of white dead nettles. The wilder accompaniments to the perennials were unplanned but they worked so I let them stay.

A clump of strawberries had positioned itself beneath one of the bulkier nine star perennials. Beneath this dense cover by mid June they were not even visible, so far withdrawn from the sunlight I did not expect them to have ripening fruit, but they did! Wild strawberries have been scattered round the garden for years and I had acquired this cultivated for the pure pleasure of eating larger fruit. Allowing them to run free they ended up in this unusual position.

Ultimately the nettles and forget-me-nots grew too strongly and were either pulled up or cut down and the cultivated strawberries proved to be too vigorous to allow in with the vegetables. These supporting plants were allowed to 'be' for a while, but when they began to become more dominant I intervened.

I am always looking for the elusive and indefinable quality of 'balance' – balance between the edible plants and those fulfilling another purpose – and balance between intervening in the garden and allowing nature to run free. This middle ground is neither a process nor a method. It is about being in close touch with the plants as the garden continues to unfold, getting down to ground level, looking regularly and intently. Having said that there are principles that can be distilled from experience and used for guidance.

A polyculture of perennial vegetables is continually evolving; you don't start each year from scratch in the same way as a conventional vegetable plot. Some plants demonstrate they are not happy and maybe others do better than expected and take up more room. Changes will always need to be made, but the aim of any and every intervention must be maintaining a balance between the food plants and the other components of the polyculture. But maintenance, although necessary is not onerous, far from it!

Principles

I have found that the most useful approach to take is to attempt to transpose the universal principles of natural farming to polycultures of perennial vegetables.

This is quite different to adopting Fukuoka's methods of natural farming; rather it is about enacting his philosophy by seeking out how to do as little as possible; not quite nothing, but ideally to intervene as little as possible.

I am certain that this approach is incredibly significant, and quite possibly vital to growing successful polycultures. The enormous number of variables that can occur means that it is impossible to predict the precise course of events or outcome. As the plan is to create an assembly of plants that will ultimately function akin to a natural ecosystem it is appropriate to stand back and to observe closely, seeking first to do nothing. But it is equally appropriate and absolutely essential that action is taken when it is required. Inevitably there will be error along with the trial, but this year's failure can be next year's success if we learn from experience.

How does this work in practice?

Influenced by Fukuoka, but with less insight than enthusiasm, I began with an ultra laid back, laissez faire attitude deliberately leaving things to go their own way as much as possible. It soon emerged that I had not taken sufficient account of the tendency of the stronger plants to crowd out others and naively I had expected everything to grow the way I had planned and hoped!

Some plants were well behaved in their first year, but became troublesome the next year when I wasn't watching them so hard or they had become larger and correspondingly stronger. For example, in their first year cultivated strawberries did well growing in small numbers around some of the brassicas, but the next year the bed nearly became a strawberry bed as they romped around swamping the other plants and swallowing up precious fertility. The lesson learned was to remove the strawberries to a pot.

Likewise mint lulled me into a false sense of security. Uncharacteristically it hardly grew for years and I convinced myself that I had the one garden that it didn't really like and therefore it would continue to stay quite small. Then one summer it took off in every direction and virtually drowned a number of the young onions. I allow it to grow where it wants but cut it back hard when picking for the kitchen or as soon as it starts to equal or exceed the height of neighbouring plants. Like a game of snakes and ladders it is then back at the beginning and never gets to win.

Forget-me-nots dot themselves round the garden, happily self-seeding in virtually every corner. Come the spring they erupt into a fabulous pale blue froth which I adore. This soft spot meant that at first I indulged them and allowed them to grow wheresoever they landed. But you can have a bit too much of a good thing and I pull many of them up. Even so there are always plenty remaining to bloom and look gorgeous.

Many wild flowers (weeds) have been welcomed in my patch, but over time woodruff, herb Robert, speedwell, nettles, woundwort and others have all begun to take over. There is no way you can predict in advance that a plant that was previously growing quietly and being useful will seemingly overnight develop megalomaniac tendencies, grow to giant proportions and start to take over. Therefore keep watch and when necessary take out or cut back anything that gets too large for its role. If possible note these happenings and retain the information for future reference.

So I learned the lesson that in a polyculture some plants will always tend to fare better than others and the only way to maintain balance is to:

• Watch closely

• Keep planned members of the polyculture to their allotted areas

• Pull out or cut down unplanned plants that are not providing any benefit

In time I may be able to add many more specific examples of one plant getting out of hand but, rather than lists of what to do when it is simpler to remember the principle that is established, watch, evaluate and take action if necessary.

Interestingly I recently read something very similar and more eloquently phrased in *The Tao of Pooh and the Te of Piglet* by Benjamin Hoff:*

"If we were asked to condense Taoist teachings regarding everyday life to their irreducible essentials we would say: Observe, Deduce and Apply. Watch what is around you – putting aside, as best you can, previous conceptions that you or others might have about it. Ideally look at it as though you were seeing it for the first time. Mentally reduce it to its basic elements, "See simplicity in complexity", as Lao-tse put it. "Use intuition as well as logic in order to understand what you see… Look for connections between one thing and another – notice patterns and relationships. Study the natural laws you see operating through them. Then work with those laws, applying the smallest possible amount of interference and effort, in order to learn more and achieve whatever you need to – and no more."

---

* *The Tao of Pooh and the Te of Piglet*; Benjamin Hoff; Egmont Books Ltd, 2002; p.324

It may take a while to begin to understand the rationale behind a more relaxed approach to what happens, but keep in mind that it is as necessary or more necessary to be alert and watchful and to know what is going on. This is of course particularly true during the rush of growth in spring.

Changing to a different way of doing things is always challenging. It was only when I started to observe my own reaction to intervening less in the garden and taking the place of an observer that it became apparent how conditioned I was to directing what happens and how hard it is to cede control and become an enabler in the garden instead.

'Weeding'

When nature does the inevitable and interposes her own additions to the garden – otherwise known as 'weeds' the choice is between taking immediate action or watching and waiting, refraining from interfering until you see what happens.

In general I opt to watch and wait, although I was wary at first about how this would work in practice. I therefore deliberately tested it by maintaining a policy of allowing dandelions, docks, nettles, and just about anything that arrived to stay if it occupied a gap, on the basis that it is better to have any plant than unused space. As all my planned perennial vegetables plants are raised separately and planted out when reasonably mature there is no competition between 'weeds' and very small seedlings. If the space the 'weed' occupies is required then it has to go, although if it is delivering an unexpected benefit it may stay for longer.

For me the journey from gardening as a series of planned tasks, to watching and waiting, taking action only when necessary has been a gentle process of transition. As I have ceded control I have found myself rejoicing in things I would once have fought against – nettles in the hedge, cleavers madly scrambling up anything and everything in spring; a spreading carpet of self heal, wild violets and creeping jenny running amongst the brassicas. The nettles are used for mulch, cleavers are easily pulled by the handful and again used as a mineral rich mulch, the self heal attracts insects, wild violets and creeping jenny provide pretty flowers and ground cover.

During the growing season it is a delight to spend time watching things grow and looking for harvests.

Here are some examples of plants that were not planned but which remain in the perennial patch to continue to grow until they impinge too much on the vegetables,

Cleavers' mad spring scramble over garlic and up raspberry canes (May).

Self-sown ground cover of self heal and next year's forget me nots growing round shallots (July).

look very untidy or set lots of unwanted seed. This includes many plants that are often regarded as real problems in the garden, so I have listed why I leave them and what I use them for:

- Stinging nettles are mineral accumulators par excellence and also provide insect habitat and nectar. Early in the year the young spring leaves make a very tasty and leaf vegetable which is especially good in soup.

- Pink and white flowering dead nettles make an attractive early year ground cover. Bees like them and they are easily pulled out when they get straggly or mildewed.

- Goose grass (cleavers) is fabulous for mineral accumulation. I generally just pull up, fold it and place it on the ground nearby.

- Rosebay willowherb is another marvellous mineral accumulator which again is easy to pull or chop the leaves off. As it is a prolific self-seeder I do not allow it to set seed.

- Toadflax is another wild plant which I spent many years trying to eradicate and marvelling at its tenacity. Young plants are easily pulled up and used for mulch. I have noticed that bees love it so I let quite a few grow for them.

- Greater celandine makes a good early year ground cover and bees like the flowers. They are prolific self-seeders so I don't let them run to seed. The sap is effective on warts but be careful it stains things and people yellow.

- Self heal is a pretty low growing ground cover during the summer months and another plant that the bees love.

- Forget-me-not is gorgeous in spring, especially as it surrounds new growth and young plants. Loved by insects looking for early flowers I pull them up towards the end of flowering. By this time they have set seed for next year. They can get too large or too prolific and I pull lots out.

- Wild violets are very pretty in spring as a ground cover. The young leaves can be eaten in salad early in the year. They mainly stay small and are cut back if they get in the way.

- Docks are mineral accumulators. Every now and again the leaves are removed and fed back to the soil as a green mulch. They are not allowed to flower and set seed. As they are regularly pulled they don't grow to huge proportions and they are confined to the wilder edges of the garden.

- Dandelions are extremely pretty in spring if you look at them as flowers and not as a problem. The seed heads attract goldfinches and bullfinches into the garden. The leaves form a rosette that does not always interfere with neighbouring plants which are easily removed and fed back to the soil as a green mulch. Some plants are growing enormous leaves which I take to be a sign of fertility and rejoice! I really do consider them an asset rather than a problem. You can make dandelion wine with the flower heads, and other parts (leaves and root) are also edible but rather strong tasting.

- Yarrow is an attractive summer flower that the insects love. It is a mineral accumulator and an aromatic pest confuser.

My resistance to using the term 'weeds' is not intended to be pedantic but is an attempt to remove a label which may prevent a huge array of lovely wild flowers and useful plants being recognised for their many benefits and uses in a polycultural garden. Neither is leaving so many uninvited guests merely indiscriminate laziness. All of the above and anything else that arrives need to be watched. Wild plants are tough and vigorous and unchecked would run amok.

Some plants are too vigorous for my garden and are removed at first sight. To date these are hedge woundwort, buttercup, clove root, viper's bugloss and any kind of grass. All gardens have different conditions and what is manageable in my garden may be a real problem in yours. Any new arrivals need to be identified and watched closely to see how they behave. Look around the neighbourhood and check if the plants appearing in your garden are running wild nearby. If they are it might be best to remove them as you will undoubtedly continue to get more.

Some plants fall between being downright useful and being a menace. In my garden they include herb Robert, evening primrose and speedwell. When there are enough to be useful any new arrivals are pretty ruthlessly removed!

I was heartened to read the following sublime description in her lovely book *The Morville Hours** where Katherine Swift describes what happened during periods of ill health and her inability to tend the garden. Her initial dismay turned to yet deeper reverence for her beloved garden as she saw the beauty of combinations she would never have planned and planted:

"Cardoons among the pinks; *Verbena bonariensis* among the seakale; huge grey woolly mulleins promising spires of yellow flowers among the purple artichokes; … colours were mingled with a breath-taking verve … And each spring I was lost in admiration: the plants did it all by themselves. I had learned to stop worrying and trust my garden."*

I too have found that leaving nature to place plants where she will, has resulted in some astoundingly attractive plant combinations that I never would have been able to design.

Mineral accumulators

A number of the plants cited above accumulate minerals and are important to building fertility, but equally they need to be watched. Other mineral accumulators, particularly those recommended for use in forest gardens will also need to be carefully monitored. Plants that can compete effectively with trees may be over vigorous in a patch of vegetables. I planted two wild chicory plants in one of the polyculture patches. In the first year they made virtually no growth and lulled me into a false sense of security. The next year they grew like mad and started to suppress the surrounding vegetables. I cut them back very hard at least twice, using the cuttings as green mulch in place. This brought things back to a more acceptable balance.

Nitrogen fixers

In similar fashion I have had some bother with white clover. I initially grew a pink clover from a pack of sprouting seeds just because I had them to hand. But because I read that white clover is a good green manure and companion for including in polycultures I sowed some this summer. I am now pulling it out. It grows far too vigorously for my patches, swamping neighbouring plants and just cannot stay. By contrast the pink clover is tall and floppy and gets in the way a bit, but can be cut back without any fuss. It does not invade and the bees love it. All nitrogen fixers can use their ability to their own advantage, so watch them!

* *The Morville Hours*; Katherine Swift; Bloomsbury Publishing, 2008; p.148-9

Nature put most of these plants in place, from left to right: wild marjoram, toad flax, dead nettle, forget me nots, columbine; I planted the blackcurrant (left), Jerusalem artichoke (centre) and elephant garlic (left of centre) (July).

Pests and disease

To a more conventional gardener there may be nothing more foolhardy than a relaxed approach to pests and disease and I completely agree. However the principles of permaculture limit the type of action that can be taken. Chemical pesticides and fungicides are firmly off limits as their use damages the ecosystem to such a degree that it is rendered more vulnerable to further pest damage. A vicious cycle is then engendered with any further use of chemicals undermining the natural health still further.

Pests

Specifically including aromatic pest confuser plants in the polyculture will repel some potentially damaging insects. Additionally a naturalistic 'ecosystem' will tend towards balance with no one species being able to establish predominance over the others. 'Pests' will still occur and may cause damage, but as they form a single link in the food chain, there is a chance that a predator will be living nearby and keep them under control. That is the theory, what is the experience?

Over the years that I have been growing perennial vegetables in polycultures there have been a few skirmishes but only one really damaging pest experience with the most infamous of butterflies – the cabbage white. In the second season they caused some minor damage to some walking stick kales. These are very tough plants and they came through the experience without a problem and I became a bit complacent.

However during the third season when the cabbage whites flew over in spring they did not stop to lay eggs. I understand that they recognise their food by sight and many of my brassicas were at that time engulfed in nettles, forget-me-nots and other plants. Complacently I thought the danger was over, but was not aware of the life cycle of this butterfly and that they would be laying eggs again in the summer. By this time I had more brassicas in the garden and they were also more visible as many of the surrounding plants had been cut back. The cabbage whites found them and laid eggs. It was not long before an army of caterpillars marched round the garden eating every brassica in sight. They attacked walking stick kale, wild cabbage, Daubenton's kale, palm tree kale, nine star perennial broccoli, Brussels sprouts, purple sprouting broccoli, collards, Chinese kale, Asturian cabbage and left most standing like mere skeletons and a few with tatters of leaf hanging on. Triumph for them and a potential disaster for the brassicas.

Throughout this unhappy attack I steadfastly resisted the temptation to intervene, wanting to know what would eventually happen. By mid September there were hardly any wisps of green on any of the plants and it was hard to believe that the caterpillars were still there eating! But they were. The walking stick kale and Daubenton's kale had less damage than other varieties, but most were mere skeletons. Happily by mid October most were growing back, some with enough leaf to begin harvesting!

This should have meant that these plants would continue to grow into the following season. However the winter of 2010 / 2011 that followed hard on the heels of their autumnal recovery decimated most of these plants. By leaving them to be eaten to such an extent I had also allowed them to be weakened. I do not know if they would have survived the winter had they been in better shape, but they certainly would have had more of a chance.

In future I will allow the nettles, pink clover, dead nettles and other plants around the brassicas to stay level with their tops for as much of the time as I can and see if that can keep butterflies at bay. If I spot any butterflies I may go so far as to cut back (and eat) the largest of the brassicas to keep them out of sight and if I find any eggs or caterpillars I will remove them.

The only other pests I have seen are aphids on purple sprouting broccoli (which I was trying to see if it would become perennial) growing into its second season and black fly on the cardoon early in the year. The aphids occurred in August alongside the caterpillars and attracted more ladybirds then I have ever seen in one place before. They arrived and feasted for weeks! The black fly on the cardoon occurred early in the year and looked very unsightly on the new growth. I did not particularly notice anything eating it, but by summer it had gone and the plant was perfectly healthy.

The other infamous pest of all gardens is the universally detested slug. My garden is edged with trees and bushes which cast a lot of shade, and it is damp in places all year round whatever the weather (I am not sure why). There are also damp, shady places under and around rocks and stones, amongst the mulch and beneath established vegetation, especially on the damp garden edges. Of course this makes for perfect slug conditions and as a result they used to seem to be everywhere. Their presence meant that any attempt at annual vegetables did not get past a few inches high; all new plants were inevitably razed to the ground by the armies lurking in the wings.

The experience with perennial vegetables has happily been very different. Although inevitably some have been found in the perennial vegetable patch, particularly when the summer turned very wet, but interestingly they have not done much damage. Some small slugs have eaten the second sprouting of heads on the previous year's cabbages and some other brassica leaves but nothing to get at all concerned about. I am speculating that this may be because the perennials are so well established that they are too tough for the slugs as I have not tried to eliminate them. It goes without saying that I have not used pellets. A couple of summers ago I tried beer traps, but these caught beneficial insects as well as slugs so I quickly gave them up and have not taken any special anti slug measures since.

There is a garden pond near the perennial patch which is home to two large frogs and a massive toad. I understand that they eat slugs so maybe that is something to do with it. I have also seen blackbirds with slugs skewered on their bills banging and bashing them into shape to be eaten. Perhaps that happy natural balance has been struck!

Disease

Disease is not something to be laid back about although happily I have not had any disease problems. I am not qualified or experienced to offer advice on plant diseases. If your plants succumb to anything worrying, look up the problem in a gardening textbook or a reliable internet site. Taking appropriate action may mean removing affected plant(s) and destroying it (them).

Conventional annual vegetable gardening does of course use crop rotation as a means of guarding against disease whereas perennial vegetables, by their nature, are fixed in place. The varied elements of a polyculture should work synergistically to promote health; and strong healthy plants are more resistant to disease than weaker specimens.

Fertility

Fertility is super important. A fully-fledged forest garden could potentially become self-sufficient in nutrients. By contrast a perennial vegetable patch is on a much smaller scale and is likely to require assistance. My aim is to enable the garden to build up as much fertility as possible from within its own boundaries and with the least amount of time and energy expended.

Time spent in the garden

As the table below shows, the busiest times in the garden are spring and early summer. I spend a relatively high amount of time on sowing seeds and taking cuttings, more than I would need to just keep the polyculture patches ticking over. This is because I am continuing to experiment with different plants and ways of doing things which always involves raising far more plants in spring than I really intend to! Management and maintenance is most necessary during and just after the spring growth spurt of all the ground cover plants. I have a mass of forget-me-nots that self-seed and lots of other ground covers that need to be cut back / pulled up in May and June.

Hours spent in garden 2012

Task	Jan	Feb	Mar	Apr	May	Jun	Jul	Aug	Sep	Oct	Nov	Dec	Total	%
Seed sowing / taking cuttings	1		4	2.5	2	3	2	1					15.5	20
Management / maintenance	2.5		4	1.25	6.75	7	1	3	0.25	0.75			26.5	35
Planting out	1.5	4		0.75	1.25	6	1.5	2	2	2			21	27
Preparation of new areas		2	2	7									11	14
Other tasks	1					0.5			1.25				2.75	4
Total	6	6	10	11.5	10	16.5	4.5	6	3.5	2.75			76.75	

In 2012 I started a new polyculture patch – I did get a gardener in to lift the turf off the lawn, and have not counted his hours here. My input consisted of the time it took to overturn those turfs, add some compost and mulch materials and then sow the area with phacelia and a few other things. It was no trouble at all and compared to more conventional ways of bringing new areas under cultivation I think that eleven hours counts as no time at all!

I know it seems hard to credit but I really did only spend the equivalent of just over ten working days actually working.

The 'do nothing' vegetable patch

Of course one of the supreme joys of gardening is to tend the garden and to feel that close connection with the earth and your beloved plants. Not digging or weeding in the conventional way does mean less time spent intervening, but in no way diminishes that experience of connectedness and bond with the garden. Less time working becomes more time available to just be in the garden, to see in closer detail what is going on and thereby strengthens the connection with the land.

Productivity

I have been measuring the productivity of the perennial patches by weighing my harvests. This was a bit haphazard in 2009-2011 but I have kept much more accurate records since January 2012. With perennial vegetables the actual amount that could be harvested is open to interpretation. Undoubtedly I could have taken more, especially more salad greens, onions and kales. I mainly failed to do so because I just did not get round to going out in the dark or after / before work etc., despite my best intentions to do so. At some point though there will be a maximum that can be taken without harming any plant's ability to continue growing healthily and strongly. Determining this will be a matter of observation and sensitivity.

The table below gives a summary of what I harvested in 2012 and came from an area no larger than 300 square feet. The potential yield from this area was much greater and was reduced by the poor results for beans and fruit in the terrible wet conditions that prevailed.

Type	Weight	Percentage of Total
Salad Greens	946g	2%
Cooking Greens	9,658g	24%
Oniony plants	1,549g	4%
Roots	20,604g	51%
Fruits	6,793g	17%
Beans (not perennials)	840g	2%
Total 2012	40,390g / 40.39kg	
Total 2011	24,900g / 24.9kg	

Given that I only spent 10 days gardening, this produce took on average 1 hour per four kilos to grow. One of the things I have become very conscious of is the amount of energy expended in food growing compared to the number of calories derived from the food. If gardening takes somewhere between 270 and 300 calories per hour[*] and there are 330kcals of energy in 1kg of kale[†] it seems to me that it may be quite easy to slip into 'negative equity' in respect of energy. It seems sensible to aim to use the least amount of energy input to grow relatively low calorie green vegetables.

Edible landscaping

To increase your food production space make the most of the garden by incorporating perennial vegetables into an entire edible landscape. Instead of garden centre shrubs for a hedge use black, red and white currants, raspberries, blueberries, gooseberries, jostaberries; or look to more unusual fruiting shrubs such as chokeberries, Juneberry, barberry, hawthorn or Nanking cherry.[‡] These will be havens for wildlife as well as lovely edible features.

In the shade of your hedge, plant wild flowers and if it is damp introduce some wild garlic. Let nature take this edge where she will. Grow beans up the hedge, if you have room to plant fruit trees grow beans up them too. The more you look the more opportunities you will see to 'edible-ise' your own patch of land. If you grow carrots or parsnips leave some to run to seed and reseed themselves for the following spring.

[*] http://caloriecount.about.com/calories-burned-digging-a153
http://caloriecount.about.com/calories-burned-gardening-a176

[†] *The Composition of Foods*, Sixth Summary Edition; McCance and Widdowson; Food Standards Agency and Institute of Food Research; 2002
[‡] *Uncommon Fruits for Every Garden*; Lee Reich; Timber Press; 2004

Resilience

Since I began the perennial vegetable experiment we have had an extremely cold dry winter (2010-2011), a very dry summer (2011), a very, very wet summer (2012) and then a very snowy cold late spring (2013). Overall it has been a mixture of different extremes compared to what we have been accustomed to think of as 'normal'. Nobody knows for certain what the future will bring in terms of weather but there seems to be consensus that continued changeability and an increased frequency of extreme events is likely.

Any form of gardening is totally dependent on having the right plant in the right place for local conditions. As it is not possible to predict what the next season's weather will be, we either have to take potluck in choosing what to grow or find plants that can cope with a demanding range of climatic conditions.

In general perennial vegetables do seem to be standing up well to these very variable conditions. They tend towards the wilder, less cultivated end of the plant spectrum and seem to be naturally more resilient than many of the vegetables we are more familiar with. At times the stress of harsh weather has made the garden look a bit sad, with wilting leaves in both summer drought and winter cold. However my photographic record shows really clearly that whatever extremes prevail that the plants bounce back afterwards with surprising vigour.

Yes, I have lost some things in difficult times and each plant has its own preferred range coping better under some circumstances and less well under others. But overall the perennial vegetable polycultures are demonstrating a remarkable degree of resilience.

A path I made to get inside the polyculture (July).

chapter 12

REFLECTION

Growing our food in conjunction with nature we
bind closer the ties that link us to our Earth.

Nearly a decade after first wondering if there was such a thing as a perennial vegetable I have completed what feels like stage one of a lifetime's journey into exploring that question. This project overall has taken a great deal of time and effort and I have tried, within the resources available to me, to leave no stone unturned in a search for answers. But now I am familiar with a wide range of perennials the time for tripping over trays of pots outside the back door, crammed with experimental vegetables is now over.

What I have found out so far has surpassed my wildest hopes and clearly demonstrated that perennial vegetables and polycultures are both practical and sensible propositions. Over time it has become clear which perennial vegetables work well here and give good crops. The garden has demonstrated what appears to be remarkable fertility in response to this concerted attempt to work alongside nature and I have marvelled at the size many of the plants have grown to. The polyculture patches produce an ample array of year round green vegetables, salad leaves and onions, plus an interesting selection of root vegetables for the autumn and winter. I will definitely continue to explore the possibilities of perennial vegetables and polycultures and in particular will be looking at how to increase and sustain the best yields.

My partner has very patiently tried cooking all the different vegetables I have grown and we have both become accustomed to eating things that a few years ago neither of us had heard of. Tentatively I asked for some feedback about all this and the reply was, "I was wary at first but now I'm delighted with the variety and freshness and especially the taste of the greens which are nothing like those in the shops, they taste alive. There's been a chance to experiment with new flavours and recipes and to add to the repertoire of basic roots like carrots and swedes. It's great that we can go away on holiday and the garden looks after itself, it looks good, vibrant and healthy. I had no idea it would work as well as it has."

Growing in polycultures is proving to be both enjoyable and labour saving. Much of the 'work' involved has been raising lots of unfamiliar plants from seed and nurturing them through the transition into the garden. Learning to let go and stop interfering in the garden has helped me to feel much more connected to nature and to trust her more. I am convinced that this is the way to achieve bounteous yields. Anyone who remains sceptical about the thought of unrestrained natural growth might like to take another look at the photographs of my beautiful, exuberant garden!

I cannot measure the additional benefits of polycultures in nurturing a healthy and biodiverse local ecology but everything around me seems healthy and vibrant and we certainly have lots of easily visible members of the ecosystem – birds, bees, hoverflies, ladybirds, other flying insects, spiders, beetles and worms.

And then there are the other, wider considerations and implications of changing how I do things. For as long as I can remember I have had a personal philosophy of simple, low impact, sustainable living. Amidst the spiralling complexities of 21st century life it is not always easy to hang onto such aspirations. I don't know about you but I feel a sense of profound powerlessness about many aspects of life today; so many choices have been removed from ordinary people, not least about our food supply.

Agriculture is industrialised and is big business and controls the vast majority of the food supply. There is discussion to be had about economies of scale, crop yields and the cost of food and I am no expert on any of these matters. However it makes me deeply unhappy that in the background vast support and complex services are currently essential to support the system. Food, the most basic of human needs makes its way from field to plate propelled by a bewilderingly complicated journey. From tractors that navigate by satellite to computer monitored and controlled picking, washing, packing and distribution processes. Then there are the labour and cost inputs to agriculture, jobs in IT to support all the computers, jobs in machine maintenance, petrol costs, refrigeration costs, costs of the buildings for packing, storage and distribution, the costs of running businesses and organisations that do these things, the agricultural legalities that have to be complied with, marketing and ultimately the supermarkets. The list could be almost endless. However did growing and distributing food develop into such an Orwellian nightmare?

Things just look and feel different from the other side (July).

But if I go into my garden and pick a few perennial greens and some salad leaves for tonight's meal, these artificial inputs vanish. Equally importantly my sense of powerlessness diminishes profoundly. There is after all something I can actually do that makes a difference and has a positive environmental outcome as well.
I think that my renewed hope is one aspect of a more positive spirit that is gently permeating society. More people are concerned about fundamental issues and are more than willing to do their part towards creating a positive, sustainable future; the Transition movement being a wonderful demonstration of this. I sense from reading many blogs and websites that many, many people also yearn for a simpler life; undoubtedly less materially rich, but with a deeper connection to each other and to the fundamentals of life. After all we are each daughters and sons of the soil. Soil, water and sunlight intricately and finely worked through the plant and animal kingdoms are what we are ultimately comprised of.

When this journey began it was purely practical. I had no idea that it would also be a journey of personal change. New ways of doing require new ways of seeing and of being. Seeing your garden, your corner of this Earth, in a new way opens up the opportunity to see the wider world in new ways. Understandings can change and new meanings emerge.

Along the way there will be harvests of hope, and possibly some of disappointment; but finally we will learn how to watch, when to leave alone, when to take action. Both the gardener and the garden can relax; we know each other and have struck a comfortable balance. We feel, and have become, closely linked with nature and her cycles and our own roots sink down deeper into life.

TABLE OF PERENNIAL VEGETABLE PLANTS

Perennial Green Vegetables

Name	Height / Width (cm)	Edible Part(s)	Harvest periods / storage	Flowers	Perennial / Annual / Other	Other Functions in a Polyculture	Propagation
Asparagus	Up to 200	Young shoots	Early spring	Female plants only (these do not crop so prolifically as males)	Perennial	Attractive foliage	Sow seed in spring or grow from purchased 'crowns'
Buckler leaf sorrel	25 x indefinite	Leaves in moderation)	Spring to autumn	Insignificant flowers in spring	Perennial	Divide established clumps, sow seed in spring, does self-seed	Mineral accumulator, ground cover
Daubenton's kale	60 x 70 variegated / 60 x 60 green	Leaves	All year round	n/a	Perennial		Take cuttings from side shoots from spring to autumn
Nine star perennial broccoli	100 x 75	Leaves, flower shoots and heads	Autumn to spring	Late spring	Perennial, for several years	Flowers attract insects	Sow seed in spring
Paul and Becky's Asturian tree cabbage	60 x 50	Leaves	Year round subject to growth		Perennial		Sow seed in spring
Sea beet	60 x 60	Leaves	Spring to autumn	Flower spikes – can be removed	Perennial		Sow seed in spring
Stinging nettle	Up to 1m	Young leaves	Spring	Late spring	Perennial	Mineral accumulator, insect habitat	No need to try to grow nettles, they will of course just come!
Walking stick kale	Up to 150 (less if growing tip pinched out) x 50	Young leaves and stems, flower shoots	Autumn to spring	Late spring	Sold as annual, can be kept as perennial	Flowers attract insects	Sow seed in spring
Wild cabbage	100 x 50+	Leaves, flower shoots and heads	Autumn to spring	Late spring	Biennial or perennial	Flowers attract insects	Sow seed in spring or take cuttings in spring
Wild rocket	60 x 60 or more in fertile ground	Leaves	Early spring to autumn, possibly winter as well	Summer	Sold as annual, reliably perennial	Flowers attract insects, ground cover	Sow seed in spring
Wood sorrel	Ground cover	Leaves	All year round	Early spring	Perennial	Ground cover	Divide existing plants

Perennial Onions

Name	Height / Width (cm)	Edible Part(s)	Harvest periods / storage	Flowers	Perennial / Annual / Other	Other Functions in a Polyculture	Propagation
Allium cepa 'Perutile'	Ground cover	All parts	Spring to autumn	n/a	Perennial		Divide clumps
Chives / giant chives	20 / 40	Leaves, flowers	Spring to autumn	Spring, summer	Perennial	Pest confuser, insect plant, mineral accumulator	Sow seed in spring, divide clumps
Few flowered leek	30	Leaf, flower, bulb	March to May	Spring	Perennial	Pest confuser, insect plant	Sow seed in spring (self-sows), divide clumps
Garlic chives	20 - 30	Leaves, flowers	Spring to autumn	Summer	Perennial	Pest confuser, insect plant	Sow seed in spring, divide clumps
Nodding wild onion	20	Leaves, flowers	Summer	Summer	Perennial	Pest confuser, insect plant	Sow seed in spring, divide clumps
Perpetual leek	20 - 30	Leaf, stem	March to May	n/a	Perennial		Divide clumps
Three cornered leek	Up to 40	Leaf, stem, flower	January to May	Spring	Perennial	Pest confuser, insect plant	Sow seed in spring (self-sows), divide clumps
Tree onion	20 - 30	Leaves, onion bulb / bulbil	Spring to autumn	n/a	Perennial	Pest confuser	Plant bulbils in autumn
Welsh onion	50 - 90	Leaves, stems, bulb	Spring to autumn	Summer	Perennial	Pest confuser	Sow seed in spring or divide established clumps
Wild garlic	30	Leaf, bud, flower, root	March to May	Late spring	Perennial	Pest confuser, insect plant	Sow seed in spring (self-sows), divide clumps

Perennial Roots and Tubers

Name	Height / Width (cm)	Edible Part(s)	Harvest periods / storage	Flowers	Perennial / Annual / Other	Other Functions in a Polyculture	Propagation
Chinese artichoke	20 - 50	Tuber	Autumn		Perennial	Ground cover	Save and replant some tubers
Earth nut pea	75 x 30	Tuber	Autumn	July to September	Perennial	Nitrogen fixer, climber, insect plant	Save seed and sow in spring, save and replant some tubers
Ground nut	Over 100	Tuber	Autumn		Perennial	Nitrogen fixer, climber	Save and replant some tubers
Jerusalem artichoke	Up to 250 x 50	Tuber	Autumn / stores through winter	Late summer / autumn	Perennial	Insect plant	Save and replant some tubers
Mashua	150	Tuber	Autumn / stores through winter	Sometimes	Perennial	Climber	Save and replant tubers
Oca	50 x 50	Tuber	Autumn / stores through winter	Sometimes	Perennial	Ground cover	Replant saved tubers in spring, sow seeds if they set (I have not done this)
Scorzonera	100 x 30	Leaf (cooked) root	Leaf – spring to summer, root – autumn	April to May	Known as an annual, I grow as perennial	Insect plant	Sow seed in spring, replant top of root plus some leaves after harvesting
Skirret	Up to 100 x 30	Root	Autumn	Summer	Perennial	Insect plant	Sow seed in spring, divide and replant the crown after harvesting roots
Yam	Up to 300	Tuber	Autumn		Perennial	Climber	If tubercles form plant these / replant the top part of the root after eating the bottom part
Yacon	Up to 160 x 50	Tuber	Autumn / stores through winter	Sometimes	Perennial	Use as a climbing frame for French beans	Save and replant tubers

Annual Vegetables Grown as Perennials

Name	Height / Width (cm)	Edible Part(s)	Harvest periods / storage	Flowers	Perennial / Annual / Other	Other Functions in a Polyculture	Propagation
Bitter cress	Ground cover	Leaves	Winter to spring	Winter / spring	Annual that self-sows	Ground cover	Allow some plants to set seed and self-sow
Dwarf curly kale	30 - 40 x 30	Leaves / flower shoots	Spring to autumn	Late spring	Sold as annual, can be kept as perennial	Will grow in some shade	Sow seed in spring, cuttings from stem in spring may take root
Garlic	20	Bulb / leaves	Harvest late summer, keep over autumn and winter	Sometimes	Known as annual grown as perennial		Divide bulbs and replant in autumn
Lamb's lettuce	Ground cover	Leaves	Winter to spring	Spring	Annual that self-sows	Ground cover	Allow some plants to set seed and self-sow
Land cress	Ground cover	Leaves	Spring to summer	Spring	Annual that self-sows	Ground cover	Allow some plants to set seed and self-sow
Leek	30	Stem	Spring to autumn	Late spring of second year	Known as annual grown as perennial	Insect plant	Sow seed or divide clumps in spring
Miner's lettuce	Ground cover	Leaves	Spring	Spring	Annual that self-sows	Ground cover	Allow some plants to set seed and self-sow
Red Russian kale	Up to 80 x 40	Leaves / flower shoots	Spring to autumn	Late spring	Sold as annual, can be kept as perennial		Sow seed in spring, cuttings from stem in spring may take root
Savoy cabbage	30 - 40 x 40	Leaves	Spring to autumn	Late spring	Sold as annual, can be kept as perennial		Sow seed in spring, cuttings from stem in spring may take root
Shallots	30	Bulb / leaves	Harvest late summer, keep over autumn and winter		Known as annual grown as perennial		Divide bulbs and replant in autumn
Spring onion	20	Stem	Spring to autumn, possibly winter	Sometimes	Known as annual grown as perennial	Ground cover	Sow seed or divide clumps in spring

SUPPLIERS OF SEEDS AND PERENNIAL VEGETABLE PLANTS

Agroforestry Research Trust / Martin Crawford

Agroforestry Research Trust, 46 Hunters Moon, Dartington, Totnes TQ9 6JT
www.agroforestry.co.uk
Supplies a very wide range of trees, bushes, perennial vegetables and seeds from the demonstration forest garden

Backyard Larder

http://backyardlarder.com/index.html
Sells small quantities of perennial vegetables raised at home and on allotment

B and T World Seeds

Paguignan, 34210 Aigues-Vives, France
+33 (0)4 68 91 29 63
http://b-and-t-world-seeds.com
A vast resource of seeds

Chiltern Seeds

Crowmarsh Battle Barns, 114 Preston Crowmarsh, Wallingford, OX10 6SL
01491 824 675
www.chilternseeds.co.uk
Fresh seeds of almost 4,000 items, many rare and unusual

Edulis

The Walled Garden, Tidmarsh Lane, Pangbourne RG8 8HT
01635 578 113 / 07802 812 781
www.edulis.co.uk
Growers of rare plants and suppliers of some perennial vegetables

Edwin Tucker

Tuckers Country Store, Brewery Meadow, Stonepark, Ashburton TQ13 7DG
01364 652 403
www.edwintucker.com
Established for 175 years and has some heirloom varieties

Eric Deloulay

Pepiniere Eric Deloulay, 1261 Rue de Cornay 45590, Saint-Cyr-En-Val, France
www.aromatiques.fr
Daubenton's kales and perpetual leek

Kings Seeds

Monks Farm, Coggeshall Road, Kelvedon, Colchester, Essex CO5 9PG
01376 570 000
www.kingsseeds.com
A wide variety of vegetable, herb and flower seeds

Magic Garden Seeds

www.magicgardenseeds.com
Supply heritage varieties

Pennard Plants

Pennard Plants, The Walled Gardens, East Pennard, Somerset BA4 6TP
01749 860 039
www.pennardplants.com
Seeds of heritage vegetables and wild and unusual plants

Plantes et Jardins

www.plantes-et-jardins.com
Daubenton's kale, perpetual leek and other perennial vegetables

Poyntzfield Herb Nursery

Poyntzfield Herb Nursery, Black Isle, By Dingwall, Ross & Cromarty IV7 8LX, Scotland
www.poyntzfieldherbs.co.uk
Mainly herbs, but have some perennial alliums

The Real Seed Company

PO Box 18, Newport, near Fishguard, Pembrokeshire SA65 0AA

01239 821 107

www.realseeds.co.uk

Heirloom and heritage vegetable seeds

Scottish Forest Garden

http://scottishforestgarden.wordpress.com/shop

Sells small quantities of seed raised on allotment

Shipton Bulbs

Y Felin, Henllan Amgoed, Whitland SA34 0SL

01994 240 125

https://shiptonbulbs.co.uk/frontpage

For wood sorrel, wild strawberry and interesting native (UK) plants

Suffolk Herbs

Suffolk Herbs, Monks Farm, Coggeshall Road, Kelvedon, Essex CO5 9PG

01376 572 456

www.suffolkherbs.com

Seeds of herbs, vegetables and wild flowers

Thomas Etty Esq

Heritage Seedsman and Bulb Merchant

Seedsman's Cottage, Puddlebridge, Horton, Ilminster, Dorset TA19 9RL

01460 298 249

www.thomasetty.co.uk

Heirloom and heritage vegetable seeds and bulbs

Victoriana Nursery

Buck Street, Challock, Ashford, Kent TN25 4DG

01233 740 529

www.victoriananursery.co.uk

Large range of vegetable seeds and plants including some perennials

BOOKS, WEBSITES AND BLOGS

BOOKS

Permaculture, forest gardens, natural farming

Creating a Forest Garden – Working with Nature to Grow Edible Crops
Martin Crawford; Green Books, Dartington, 2010

Gaia's Garden, a Guide to Home-Scale Permaculture
Toby Hemenway; Chelsea Green Publishing Company, Vermont, 2000

The Earth Care Manual – A Permaculture Handbook for Britain and Other Temperate Climates
Patrick Whitefield; Permanent Publications, Hampshire, 2004

Edible Forest Gardens – Ecological Vision and Theory for Temperate Climate Permaculture, Volume One: Vision and Theory
David Jacke with Eric Toensmeier; Chelsea Green Publishing Company, Vermont, 2005

Edible Forest Gardens – Ecological Vision and Theory for Temperate Climate Permaculture, Volume Two: Design and Practice
David Jacke with Eric Toensmeier, Chelsea Green Publishing Company, Vermont, 2005

The Edible Garden – How to Have Your Garden and Eat It
Alys Fowler, BBC Books Gardeners' World 2010

Designing and Maintaining Your Edible Landscape Naturally
Robert Kourik; Permanent Publications, Hampshire, 2004

Food From Your Forest Garden – How to Harvest, Cook and Preserve Your Forest Garden Produce
Martin Crawford and Caroline Aitken; Green Books, Dartington, 2013

How to Grow Perennial Vegetables – Low-maintenance, Low-impact Vegetable Gardening
Martin Crawford; Green Books, Dartington, 2012

How to Make a Forest Garden
Patrick Whitefield; Permanent Publications, Hampshire, 2002

The One-Straw Revolution
Masanobu Fukuoka; New York Review Books, New York, 1978; reprinted 2009 with updated preface

Paradise Lot – Two Plant Geeks, One-Tenth of an Acre, and the Making of an Edible Garden Oasis in the City
Eric Toensmeier and Jonathan Bates; Chelsea Green Publishing Company, Vermont, 2013

Perennial Vegetables
Eric Toensmeier, Chelsea Green Publishing Company, Vermont, 2007

Plants for a Future
Ken Fern; Permanent Publications, Hampshire, 1997

Sepp Holzer's Permaculture – A Practical Guide for Farmers, Smallholders and Gardeners
Sepp Holzer; Permanent Publications, Hampshire, 2010

Other interesting and informative titles

Eat Your Veg
Arthur Potts Dawson; Mitchell Beazley, London 2012
A lovely recipe book brimming with ideas. Mostly for traditional vegetables but as it is helpfully divided into sections for roots and tubers, bulbs and stems, leaves and flowers, perennial vegetables can readily be substituted into the recipes.

Lean Logic – A Dictionary for the Future and How to Survive It
David Fleming, 2011

The Power of Just Doing Stuff – How Local Action Can Change the World
Rob Hopkins; Green Books, Dartington, 2013

The Tao of Pooh and the Te of Piglet
Benjamin Hoff; Egmont Books, London, 2002

The Transition Companion – Making Your Community More Resilient in Uncertain Times
Rob Hopkins, Green Books, Dartington, 2011

The Transition Handbook – From Oil Dependency to Local Resilience
Rob Hopkins, Green Books, Dartington, 2008

Uncommon Fruits for Every Garden
Lee Reich, Timber Press, Portland, Cambridge 2004

Wild Fermentation – The Flavor, Nutrition and Craft of Live-culture Foods
Sandor Ellix Katz; Chelsea Green Publishing Company, Vermont, 2003
Another possibility for dealing with perennial kale is to ferment it in a sauerkraut
or kimchi and this book shows you how. It also describes many more fascinating
ferments and mouth-watering recipes.

Wild Garlic and Gooseberries … and Me – A Chef's Stories and Recipes from the Land
Denis Cotter; Collins, London, 2007
This is much more than a recipe book. Denis Cotter enthuses about the little
known vegetables he is passionate about. He has devised mouth-watering recipes
for perennials such as wild garlic, nettles, dandelion as well as oca, Jerusalem
artichoke, sea kale, asparagus, black and red kales and scorzonera. If you need some
inspiration for cooking your perennials – this is it!

WEBSITES AND BLOGS

My blog is kept up to date with what I am working on at present:
http://annisveggies.wordpress.com

Adaptive Seeds
www.adaptiveseeds.com/content/about-adaptive-seeds
They steward and disseminate rare, diverse and resilient seed varieties for
ecologically-minded farmers, gardeners and seed savers.

Agroforestry Research Trust
www.agroforestry.co.uk
The Agroforestry Research Trust is a non-profit making charity which researches
into temperate agroforestry and into all aspects of plant cropping and uses, with a
focus on tree, shrub and perennial crops. The website has a massive plant and seed
catalogue plus details of how to join the Forest Garden Network.

Backyard Larder Blog
http://backyardlarder.blogspot.co.uk
Exploring the possibilities of the perennial vegetable garden.

Blogger Seed Network
http://bifurcatedcarrots.eu/seed-exchange
Blog with links to an international seed saving and exchange network.

Emma Lawrence
www.emmalawrence.com
Emma drew the illustrations in this book.

Growing Oca
http://oca-testbed.blogspot.co.uk
This is a blog about just that, but also other roots such as mashua. It contains an
amazing amount of detail.

Landed
http://landed.weebly.com/forest-gardening-for-the-future.html
A detailed web site / blog about a forest garden in an average sized back garden with
lots of background information and details of how the garden has developed over
time. The aim of the blog and website is to make forest gardening, particularly at
this scale, better known and more accessible. Reading this blog is a must for anyone
contemplating guiding their back garden in this direction.

Of Plums and Pignuts
http://scottishforestgarden.wordpress.com
Another interesting and informative blog about a forest garden in Scotland.

Permaculture Magazine
www.permaculture.co.uk
Practical features, solutions, news and all things permaculture to inspire self-
reliance.

Permaculture Association
www.permaculture.org.uk

Radix for Roots
http://radix4roots.blogspot.com
A super blog about every kind of root vegetable imaginable. This wonderful array
of possibilities includes many of my favourite perennials, some I am keen to try
and lots that are currently off my radar entirely. It is full of scientific exploration and
thoughtful discussion.

Seed Ambassadors Project
http://seedambassadors.org
A sister project to Adaptive Seeds above.

Sustainable Smallholding
http://sustainablesmallholding.org
The sustainable smallholding is based on permaculture principles and is a demonstration site for the UK Permaculture Association through the LAND project. The blog is thoughtful and informative with an aim of passing on tried and tested sustainable practices.

Transition Culture
http://transitionnetwork.org/blogs/rob-hopkins
Rob Hopkins' blog.

Transition Network
www.transitionnetwork.org
The hub of the transition network with links to local initiatives round the world. Packed full of interest and inspiration.

appendix 4

DYNAMIC ACCUMULATOR PLANTS

This table relates to perennial vegetables and other plants I have in polycultures supporting them. Data is derived from the USDA database of nutrients.

Plant	Ca	K	Mg	Na	Fe	Zn	Cu	B	Se	Mn	Si
Beet Greens		Y	Y	Y	Y						
Broccoli	Y	Y			Y						
Chicory leaves	Y	Y			Y				Y	Y	
Chives	Y	Y	Y		Y	Y			Y	Y	
Cleavers	Y										
Comfrey	Y	Y	Y								
Corn salad		Y			Y		Y		Y	Y	
Dandelion leaves	Y	Y	Y	Y	Y				Y		
Dock leaves		Y	Y		Y				Y		
Garlic	Y	Y				Y			Y		
Nettles	Y	Y									
Rocket	Y										
Rosebay willow herb	Y	Y	Y		Y	Y				Y	
Spinach	Y	Y			Y	Y			Y	Y	

Source: U.S. Department of Agriculture, Agricultural Research Service. 2011. USDA National Nutrient Database for Standard Reference, Release 24. Nutrient Data Laboratory Home Page, www.ars.usda.gov/ba/bhnrc/ndl

ENZYME CO-FACTORS IN PHYSIOLOGICAL PROCESSES

Minerals are a vital part of our diet and they are well supplied in plant foods. One vital way in which the body uses them is to form enzymes that are essential to health. A few examples of enzymes that require micro minerals are listed below to give an indication of the pivotal roles they play. All of these micro minerals are to be found in kale, onions, leeks and garlic (McCance and Widdowson, *The Composition of Foods* 2002). Data is not currently available about perennial members of the kale and onion families, but they are likely to have similar constituents to their annual counterparts.

Copper
- Cupric cytochrome oxidase – this is used in the oxidation of food to produce energy.
- DNA polymerase – this is used in the process of DNA replication which is a fundamental process underpinning body repair, the generation of immune system cells, reproduction.

Iron
- Ferrous / ferric cytochrome – this is used to transfer electrons within the cells and is an integral part of energy generation.

Magnesium
- Glucose 6-phosphatase – this enzyme hydrolyses glucose-6-phosphate, which is the final step in gluconeogenesis (generating glucose from non carbohydrates) and glycogenolysis (the conversion of glycogen to glucose). These reactions raise blood sugar when required to do so.

Manganese
- Arginase – a stage in urea cycle which is for the processing and disposal of harmful ammonia.

Selenium
- Glutathione peroxidase – This is a whole family of enzymes which protect the body from oxidative damage.

Zinc
- Alcohol dehydrogenase – this is a group of enzymes which act to break down alcohol which is toxic to the body, into aldehyde, ketone and alcohol groups (a single oxygen and single hydrogen molecule linked together, not the whole compound) which are useful intermediates in a host of biochemical reactions.
- Carbonic anhydrase – this enzyme helps in the interconversion of carbon dioxide and bicarbonates, assisting carbon dioxide out of the body and helping to maintain the correct acid / base balance in the body.
- DNA polymerase – see above for magnesium.

INDEX

additional yields, principle of 21
alfalfa 34, 119
annual greens, grown as
  perennials 78-81
annual lupin 120
annual plants 11
  grown as perennials 75-78
annual roots, grown as
  perennials 81-82
annual vegetables, grown as
  perennials 151
antioxidants 45
aromatic pest confusers 40, 41,
  135-137
arthropods 30
asparagus 52-53, 113
asphodel 91
Asturian tree cabbage 49
Ayurveda 35

Babington's leek 82-83
bacteria 29, 33
bamboo 22
barley 23, 24
bee balm 104
beetles 28, 30, 41
beetroot 11
biennial plants 11
biomass 21
black fly 137
borage 91
breadroot 86
buckler leaved sorrel 53-54
buckwheat 120
burdock 81
butterflies 46, 52, 54, 69, 136

cabbage family
  Asturian tree cabbage 49
  Daubenton's kale 47-48
  nine star perennial broccoli
    48-49
  walking stick kale 49-50
  wild cabbage 50-51
cabbage whites (butterfly) 46,
  52, 54, 69, 136
calorific value,
  of the vegetables 16

campanula 91
cancer 45
cardoon plant 83, 134, 137
carrots 11, 81
cauliflower 48
centipedes 28, 30
chicory 38, 40, 100
Chinese artichoke 64-65, 77,
  114
Chinese kale 83, 136
chives 56-57, 91
claytonia 41
cleavers 107
climate change 12, 25
climbers and vines 20, 107-108
clover 34, 104
cloves 76
collards 86-7
comfrey 34, 38, 41, 100
compost 23, 28, 53, 72, 89, 118,
  122-124, 139
conifers 6
coppiced hazel 22
Crawford, Martin 21-22
Creating A Forest Gardening
  (Martin Crawford) 21-22
creeping Jenny 104, 114
crimson clover 120
crops, methods of cultivating 23

dandelion 34, 38, 40, 91, 104,
  114, 121, 133
Daubenton's kale 45, 46, 47-48,
  59, 128, 136
diseases, plant 137-138
dock 102, 133
'do nothing' vegetable patch
  139
dwarf curly kale 78-79
dynamic accumulator plants
  160

'Earth care', principle of 19
earthnut pea 65-66, 77, 109
earthworms 30
edible forest gardens 1-2, 20-22
edible landscaping 140
edible plants 21

ehrwiger kohl 51
energy conservation, in food
  production 15-16
enzyme co-factors,
  in physiological processes
    161-162
everlasting onion 57

fair shares, principle of 19
farming
  'do nothing' farming 23
  natural farming 22-24
fennel 40, 100, 114
fenugreek 120
fertilisers, chemical 34
feverfew 105
few flowered leek 57-58, 149
field beans 120
flatulence 68
flowers 109
  edible 91
food chain 28
food plants 11
food prices 5
food production 25
food webs 118
  dead 32
  living 32-33
  soil 32, 34
forest gardens 24-25, 115,
  124-125
  concept of 2
  ecological diversity 20
  edible forest gardens, see
    edible forest gardens
  layering of space in 21
  time spent in 138-139
  vegetation in 20
forget-me-nots 112, 128-129,
  132-133, 136, 138
fossil fuels 25
foxglove (Digitalis species) 100
frogs and toads 137
fructo-oligosaccharide 68
fruit trees 124-125
Fukuoka, Masanobu 22-24
  methods of natural farming
    129

gardens
  'back' garden 6, 10
  community gardens 25
  forest gardens, *see* forest
    gardens
  'front' garden 10
garden share schemes 25
garlic chives 58, 91, 149
giant chives 57, 149
glucosinolates 45
goat willow 6
Good King Henry plant 13, 87
goose grass 132
grape (*Vitis* species) 108
greater celandine 132
green manure 34, 109, 112,
  118-120, 124, 134
green vegetables
  asparagus 52-53
  Buckler leaved sorrel 53-54
  sea beet 54
  stinging nettle 54-55
  table of 148
  wood sorrel 55
groundnut 66-67, 109

hairy bittercress 80
Hart, Robert 20-22
hazel tree 6
herbaceous plants 20-22
honey bees 38, 132
hop 108
horseradish 102
horticulture 5, 13
humus 28, 33

indoles 45
insect habitat 40-1
isothiocyanates 45
ivy 108

Jerusalem artichoke 52, 66,
  67-68, 112, 114, 125

kales, perennial 45
  wild rocket 51-52
King's spear 83-85
komatsuma (Japanese mustard
  spinach) 87

ladybirds 28, 41
lamb's lettuce 41, 80
land cress 80

leek 76-77
lemon balm 102, 114
lily white 86
'live food web' 12
lovage 13, 87-88

manure, green 34
mashua 68-69
Maximillian sunflower 88
medicinal herbs 22
microorganisms 121
millipedes 28, 30
mineral accumulating plants
  38, 134
miner's lettuce 81
mint 102
mites 30
monoculture 21
monster berberis 6
mustard 120

natural farming, principles of
  128-129
nectary plants 38, 40
nematodes 30
nettles 28, 38, 41, 54, 103, 112,
  114, 124, 128, 130-132, 136, 157
nine star perennial broccoli
  48-49
nitrogen fixation 37, 67
nitrogen fixing plants 38, 41, 66,
  109, 119, 134
nodding wild onion 58, 149
nutrients cycle 30
nutrients for plants 33
nutritional tables 16

oca 69-70, 114, 125
One-Straw Revolution, The
  (Masanobu Fukuoka) 23-24
onions, perennial
  chives 56-57, 113
  everlasting onion 57
  few flowered leek 57-58
  garlic chives 58
  health benefits 56
  nodding wild onion 58-59
  perpetual leek (poireau
    perpétue) 59
  shallots 113
  table of 149
  three cornered leek 59-60
  tree onion 60, 113

  Welsh onion 60-63, 113
  wild garlic 63

parsnip 11, 81-82
peak oil 25
people care, principle of 19-20
perennial fruiting 13
perennial lettuce 88
perennial vegetables 2-3, 5-6,
  37
  advantages 11-12
  availability of 47
  brassicas, care of 46-47
  cabbage family, *see* cabbage
    family
  disadvantages 13
  finding and growing of 13-15
  gardener's part 33-35
  green vegetables, *see* green
    vegetables
  guiding principles and aims
    15-17
  leafy greens and shoots 45-47
  onions, *see* onions, perennial
  perennial kales, *see* kales,
    perennial
  recipes using, *see* recipes,
    using perennials vegetables
  resilience of 141
  right nutrients for 33
  roots and tubers, *see* roots
    and tubers
  selection of 44
  site for growing, *see* site
    for growing, perennial
    vegetables
  suppliers of 152-154
permaculture 19-20
  edible forest gardening 20-22
  Fukuoka, Masanobu 22-24
  perennial vegetables, growing
    of 22
perpetual leek (poireau
  perpétuel) 59
pests 135-137
phacelia 120
phytonutrients 52
'phytonutrients' lutein 45
pig nut 85
pink clover 114
plants
  diversity 12
  ground cover and low plants

104-107
medium height plant 102-103
nutrients for 33
pathology 22
raising from seed 123-124
size, shape and form 41
tall plants 100-101
podding vegetables 13
polycultures 2-3, 6, 10, 15, 20,
33-34, 53, 71, 78, 99
advantages of 38
edible polycultures, creation
of 113-115
elements of 38-41
maintaining of balance
between the edible plants
127-128
meaning of 37
natural farming, principles of
129-131
planning for 113-115
'potted polycultures' 11, 125
size and scale 115
starting points and general
principles 111-112, 128-129
theory and practice of 17
weeding 131-134
'potted polycultures' 11, 125
predators 21, 40
productivity, of perennial
patches 139-140
protozoa 29-30
purple sprouting broccoli 79
purpletop vervain 109

recipes, using perennials vegetables
chickpea and kale soup 94-95
kale and leek colcannon 95
kale with ginger, garlic and
chilli 96
roasted perennial root
vegetables 97
wild rocket soup 97
red clover 91, 119
'Red Russian' kale 80, 151
rice 23, 24
roots and tubers 112
Chinese artichoke 64-65, 114
Earth Nut Pea 65-66
groundnut 66-67
Jerusalem Artichoke 67-68
mashua 68-69
oca 69-70

scorzonera 70-71
skirret 71-72
table of 150
yacon 72-73
yam, Chinese 73
yam, Japanese 73
rosebay willowherb 101, 132

salad burnet 13, 89
salsify 81
savoy cabbage 79
scorzonera 70-71, 81
sea beet 54
sea holly 85
sea kale 85-86
self heal 132
shallots 77
sheet mulching 118
site for growing, perennial
vegetables
fruit trees, bushes and forest
gardens 124-125
patch and ongoing fertility,
establishing of 121-123
preparation of, and initial
fertility 118-119
raising plants from seed
123-124
selection of 117
skirret 71-72, 114
slugs 6, 137
soil condition 28-30
soil fertility 12, 16, 38, 60, 118,
121, 138
soil food webs 32, 34
soil fungi 29
soil life cycle 30
soil structure 32
assimilation horizon 27
banking layer 28
basics of 27-28
eluviation layer 28
organic horizon 27
sorrel 89
spiders 28, 30, 41
spinach 89
spinach beet 89
spring onions 77-78
stinging nettles 54-55, 103, 132,
148
storing, of perennial vegetables
125
sunlight 10, 21, 33, 41, 45

suppliers, of perennial
vegetables 152-154
Sutherland kale 79, 80
swede 11
sweet cicely 103

tares 120
tartar bread plant 86
Taunton Dean (British plant) 51
temperate forests 21
three cornered leek 59-60
thyme (Thymus species) 105, 114
tiger nut 89
toadflax 132
Traditional Chinese Medicine
34-35
Trail of Tears French bean 72,
109, 125
Transition Movement (2006)
24-25, 146
tree canopy 20-21, 41
tree onion 60
trefoil 120
Trouve Tronchuda plant 51
tubers, underground 66

violet (Viola species) 105

walking stick kale 49-50
wallflowers 75
web of life, concept of 32
weeding 131-134
weeds 28
Welsh onion 60-63
white clover 119
wild arjoram 103
wild cabbage 50-51
wild chicory 34
wild garlic 63, 91
wild marjoram 103, 115, 135
wild rocket 51-52
wild strawberry 105, 112, 115
wild vegetables 11
wild violet 115, 133
wood lice 28
wood sorrel 55

yacon 72-73
Yam, Chinese 73
Yam, Japanese 73
yarrow 105, 115, 133

zeaxanthin 45

SUBSCRIBE
to *the*
sustainable living magazine

Permaculture magazine offers tried and tested ways of
creating flexible, low cost approaches to sustainable living

BE INSPIRED by practical solutions and ideas

SAVE on our exclusive subscriber offers

FREE home delivery – never miss an issue

HELP US SUPPORT permaculture projects
in places with no access to currency

SUBSCRIBE, CHECK OUR DAILY UPDATES
AND JOIN THE PERMACULTURE ENEWSLETTER TO RECEIVE SPECIAL
OFFERS ON NEW AND EXISTING BOOKS, TOOLS AND PRODUCTS:

www.permaculture.co.uk

Enjoyed this book?

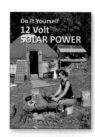

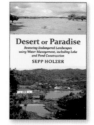

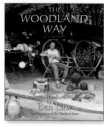

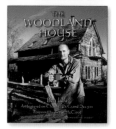

SIGN UP TO THE PERMANENT PUBLICATIONS ENEWSLETTER
TO RECEIVE NEWS OF NEW TITLES AND SPECIAL OFFERS:

www.permanentpublications.co.uk